*"By means of the Olympic Games
sport has conquered the whole world.
From now on—though the flame may flicker
or even go out in some places—
it will surely continue to shine elsewhere,
until it is lit again where it once shone before"*

Baron Pierre de Coubertin, founder of the modern Olympics

GOLDEN MOMENTS

A Collection of United States 1984 Commemorative Olympic Issues

Foreword by James A. Michener

Paintings and 1984 Olympic postage designs by Robert Peak

Published by the United States Postal Service, Washington, D.C., 1984

The U.S. Postal Service is very pleased to dedicate this book to the late Jim Thorpe—a superb athlete and proud American who embodied the finest elements of the Olympic Games.

When Thorpe won both the decathlon and pentathlon in the 1912 Olympics by huge margins over his nearest rivals, King Gustav V of Sweden said: "You, sir, are the world's greatest athlete." In 1950, an Associated Press poll named Thorpe "Greatest Male Athlete" of the first half of the 20th Century.

To the Sac and Fox Tribe member whose Indian name meant "Bright Path," we salute your memory and accomplishments on these pages.

William F. Bolger
Postmaster General

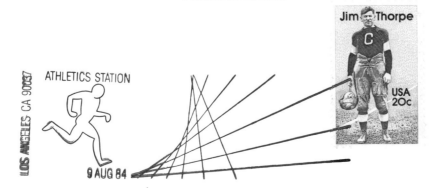

Foreword

by James A. Michener

A chief pleasure of my life is serving on the Citizens' Stamp Advisory Committee, an assembly of 17 men and women who counsel the Postmaster General on policy in issuing United States stamps. We do not decide which stamps shall be printed; that final decision remains in the hands of the Postmaster General. We merely advise.

But when it has been agreed by all involved that a new series, an appropriate block, or a single commemorative is required, we assume reponsibility for seeing that the content is accurate, that a good designer is employed and that an artistic, pleasing result is achieved. The high reputation which United States stamps enjoy throughout the philatelic world is due in part to the severe attention we try to pay to their production. Far too often drab stamps slip by, but we also produce many little masterpieces of which the nation can be proud and which collectors can be happy to own.

It was with some excitement that our Committee learned, several years ago, that in 1983 we would begin issuing a master set of 24 stamps plus four pieces of postal stationery to honor our nation's hosting the 1984 Summer Olympic Games. We were charged with bringing forth a varied, accurate, colorful and appealing set of stamps which would represent the excitement and challenge of these games.

At the start we made a series of important decisions. First: "It won't be all running and jumping." Second: "Winter and summer will be represented." Third: "The activities represented will be as accurately depicted as possible." Fourth: "They will be well designed." Fifth: "They will be colorful."

With this sizable obligation ahead of us, I started reviewing how stamps had been utilized in previous years and I found that from 1896 through 1960 alone, 564 Olympic stamps had been issued showing specific events like running and discus, plus another 131 honoring the games themselves but without depicting specific events. Since then the number of issues has approached a thousand.

The series was handsomely launched in 1896 when the ancient games, which had run from 776 B.C. to A.D. 393, when Roman Emperor Theodosius halted them for religious reasons and tore up the stadiums, were revived as the result of agitation ignited by the French enthusiast, Baron de Coubertin. The revival was held in Athens, and to celebrate it Greece issued a series of 12 stamps, beautifully designed, abominably printed, of which the one drachma showed the ancient Olympic stadium in Athens, which has been elegantly restored.

The 25 lepta showed a four-horse chariot race and, as I studied the art of these stamps of 1896, I wondered whether we could do as well in 1984.

In 1906 the 10th anniversary of the renewal was celebrated, again in Athens and again with a series of 14 much better printed stamps of equally high design. The three drachma showed four runners borrowed from a vase dating back to the original games.

Greece's happy idea of issuing stamps coincident with the Games did not immediately catch on, for the Paris Games of 1900, St. Louis of 1904, London of 1908 and Stockholm of 1912 provided not one Olympic stamp among them, and World War I obliterated the games in 1916. But in 1920 the Antwerp Games were honored when Belgium of-

fered a handsomely designed series of three classic designs. The five centimes utilized the famous statue Discobolus which the Greek sculptor Myron did in 450 B.C.

The floodgates were now opened, with host nations vying for the honor of producing the best and most innovative stamps. Some of the changes were commendable, as when France in 1924 issued four, some of which showed modern French scenes, or when Uruguay in 1924 issued a stamp to celebrate her football (soccer) victory. However, I can cite three examples of experiments which did not succeed: The Netherlands 1928 series, which used only modern design; the Portugal issue of that same year, which used for the first time the Olympic interlocking rings, and the United States stamp of 1932, which first recognized the Winter Games.

In succeeding years the collector had hundreds of Olympic stamps from which to choose, and some of the triumphs should be honored, for they provided little masterpieces of art, movement, color and sports competition.

The most successful Olympic stamp ever issued, in the judgment of many including this writer, was also one of the most moving. It was issued by Switzerland in 1944, when the world was rocked by war, and recalled in that dreadful time the glories of peaceful competition. The series of three two-color stamps reproduced a statue of Apollo carved about 460 B.C. and uncovered in modern times. It is framed on four sides

by superb lettering, and the five circles are appropriately placed. The 20 centime value is about as fine a stamp as could be designed and printed.

For similar reasons I like the Saar issue of 1956 and the austere Federal Republic of Germany stamp of 1972, which combines excellent design, good lettering and a strong symbolic figure. The Italian stamp of 1960 showing the tired boxer Kleitomachos is good, but the stamp which best catches both

the art and the athlete is the Canadian issue of 1975 in which a contemporary statue by the American sports sculptor, R. Tait McKenzie, shows a sprinter in the starting blocks.

These were excellent primarily because they used works of art to create a sense of dignity and participation, a good point for designers to remember. Now, however, with the aid of photography, high-speed cameras, and more effective printing processes, it became possible for nations to issue sports stamps which were sometimes breathtakingly beautiful and effective. My favorite is the Czechoslovakian issue of 1960 showing two sprinters taking off at the gun. This is a magnificent stamp, a perfect marriage of design, lettering, background and powerful imagery. Almost equally effective were the splendid German Olympic stamps of 1935-36 whose elegant

design and beautiful printing showed what could be accomplished in this field. The 12 pfennig was one of the best, although each of the other 10 was a little gem. Norway's series of 1951 provided three exceptionally good representations of winter sports, while the vigorous winter stamps of Austria in 1963 combined good art, fine lettering and strong printing.

I liked especially the 25 mark value in Finland's 1952 issue, for it showed a modern runner, powerfully drawn, against a background frieze of four runners taken from an ancient vase. But I was also pleased by the totally modern effect of the Japanese 50 yen stamp of 1972 show-

ing skaters against a blue sky and the barest suggestion of the Sapporo arena in which the Winter Games were to be held.

But as I studied the Olympic stamps I also began to note issues that would serve to remind our committee of what to avoid. High on the list were three stamps offering symbolic designs, not automatically a bad idea if the designs are appropriate and artistically executed. The one shilling Great Britain issue of 1948, showing Victory skipping across the Atlantic to commemorate the fortunate outcome of World War II, would fall in that category. Even worse, I thought, was that Portugese stamp on which the

five circles first appeared. If requested, I could point out seven unsettling elements in this stamp, not the least being the "wings" coming out of the hurdler's shoulderblades. But I would also cite the Australian two shilling issue of 1955 as an example of intemperate design. I contend that the lettering is confusing and pointless, the five rings are not well utilized, and the coat-of-arms of Melbourne, the city hosting the Games, is totally ineffective.

Other stamps were bad because they misused not design but sports. The Federal Republic of Germany 30 pfennig of 1972 showing basketball does not rep-

resent the game well, while the Netherlands series of 1928 garnered a kind of championship by presenting eight different sports, each in grossly improper form. My nomination for one of the worst representations of the athlete is the 10-cent stamp of this series showing a runner like none seen before or since.

And like many a philatelist

before me, I objected also to those stamps often issued by smaller countries to gain support *from* the Olympics rather than to lend aid *to* them, such as the Dominican Republic issue of 1958 showing little more than a photograph of Charles Jenkins and Tom Courtney of the United States exchanging the baton in 1956. I do not argue with those collectors who question whether this flood of Olympic winners from the Dominican Republic, 32 in all, should be counted among authentic Olympic stamps.

Up to now I've cited with perfect hindsight only the regretful issues of other countries. And here the United States did not escape. Between 1932, when we issued our first Olympic stamp, to 1980, we had offered 22 stamps (not including stationery), none having caused more furor than the famous first, which appeared in 1932 to honor the Winter Olym-

pics held that year at Lake Placid. The background showing the Adirondacks wasn't bad, but the four types of lettering were both too much and too undistinguished. However, it was that skier who gave the trouble! He appears to be making a leap through the air while carrying poles, a feat which caused observers at the time to cry: 'He's about to kill him-

self!' When defenders argued that he was really on a cross-hill run, the critics still protested: 'If he is, he's going to break both legs and maybe an arm.' Pudgy, unathletic, poorly drawn, improperly clothed, the skier became a philatelic monstrosity and the stamp the poorest Olympic ever issued by the United States.

Since then our nation has produced several quite

handsome works. Our second in the series, issued for the Summer Games in 1932, placed the figure of a runner within the traditional and handsome frame devised for the ordinary postage stamp series of 1922-25, and the 1976 issues showed how simplified art can be used with great effectiveness. However, that same style produced a massively heavy figure skater nicknamed "Miss Butterball of 1976."

With these artistic criteria in mind, I looked at the noble roster of Olympic heroes and heroines and found that five were almost universally conceded to have been heroic in their performances: Paavo Nurmi, the unbeatable Flying Finn who won nine gold medals in grueling distance races; Al Oerter who won a gold medal for the discus in each of four successive Olympics; Fanny Blankers-Koen, the astonishing Dutch woman who won four golds in 1948; Jesse Owens who won four golds at the Berlin games in 1936, to Hitler's disgust; and Mark Spitz who won an incredible seven golds in eight days in Munich in 1972.

There may have been a sixth superman, a shadowy American jumper named Ray Ewry, who seems to have won eight gold medals starting in 1900 when the competition was feeble and the organization poor.

There were also sentimental and popular winners worthy of being honored on stamps. Nadia Comaneci, the Romanian in 1976, and Olga Korbut, the Russian in 1972, were immensely applauded as the darlings of their Games. Babe Didrikson (Zaharias) had been outstanding with two gold medals; she was robbed of a third by the judges and had the rules of that time permitted women to compete in more than three events she might well have won six or seven. In a major meet just prior to the Olympics this 17-year-old Texas girl had won first place in the shot put, the javelin, the broad jump, the baseball throw and the 80-meter hurdles, with a tie for high jump and a fourth in discus.

In one year, 1912, Jim Thorpe won both the pentathlon and the decathlon, a prodigious feat, and in 1960 the graceful Wilma Rudolph garnered three golds. Three of the handsomest young men ever to compete were also three of the most popular winners: Lord Burghley, now Marquis of Exeter, in the 1928 high hurdles, Jean-Claude Killy in 1968 skiing, and Bruce Jenner in the 1976 decathlon. Duke Kahanamoku, the great Hawaiian swimmer, was also immensely popular.

The records show some surprises, too. Joe Frazier and Cassius Clay (Muhammad Ali) both won gold medals in boxing, as did Senator Bill Bradley and Bill Russell in basketball. But one of the most memorable winners did not win a gold. When the Games were held in Stockholm in 1912, the Swedes insisted upon holding a military pentathlon featuring riding and shooting, and because they had trained so ardently for it, they won the first four places and would have won the fifth had they been

allowed that many entries. Who was the fifth medalist? A young American cavalry officer named George S. Patton, who pursued his military training to World War II immortality.

Why have not these notable winners been honored on our stamps? Surely many deserve the honor. But a firm and reasonable rule of the Postal Service says that no living person shall appear on an American stamp and that no dead person may appear, excepting former Presidents, until 10 years have elapsed since death. This excellent provision has kept our stamps from being cluttered with minor figures, but it caused something of a scandal with our second Olympic stamp. In 1932 designer V. S. McCloskey modeled the runner too closely upon a photograph of the California athlete J. A. LeConey, so just as the stamp was about to appear the face had to be redrawn. Today's artists are warned not to repeat that error.

Because of this strict rule only two of our Olympic heroes have qualified: Babe Didrikson Zaharias, honored in 1981, and Jim Thorpe, honored in 1984. We can suppose that others will join them as they become eligible.

One hopes that it will be many years before such stars as Al Oerter, Wilma Rudolph and Tenley Albright become eligible. But at the next meeting of our committee I'm going to start a campaign for this fellow Ray Ewry, because anyone who can win eight gold medals in anything deserves remembrance.

With such background material to guide it, the Postal Service decided to issue a set of 24 beautiful stamps plus four items of postal stationery to honor the Los Angeles Summer Games and the Sarajevo Winter ones. Was this too many? Was this an unwarranted emphasis on sports?

Baron de Coubertin, in reviving the games, said that he thought nations which excelled in sports excelled in other aspects of national life. The Duke of Wellington believed that his victory at Waterloo was made possible by young men who had been trained in hard games at Eton. Certainly, America loves games, but not yet excessively. We do not compare in over-emphasis with South Africa, Brazil or Australia. And we host the Olympics only rarely.

When our committee planned the series we sought athletic authenticity, diversity, movement, drama, excellent drawing and vivid color. With artist Bob Peak's practiced skill, I think we achieved it. The vertical blocks of four are exceptionally good, and I am pleased to see that we have included certain sports in which we do not traditionally excel, such as soccer and cycling. The ice dancing pair is a masterpiece, and I prize the girl gymnast with her toes arched over her head, or the male diver about to straighten out. I like the design of the weight lifter and the tension shown by the discus thrower. To show the pole vaulter in a horizontal stamp is both unique and pleasing.

What in the future? One would like to see a block of four honoring past greats like Nurmi, Oerter, Rudolph and Blankers-Koen, but thankfully considering U.S. policy about living persons on stamps, this won't happen any time soon. Olympic stars tend to be young and they live a long time. It will be well into the next century before we can honor the divine Comaneci, or the gracious Jean-Claude Killy, or the dazzling Mark Spitz, or the dryad-like Wilma Rudolph whom the Italian press called "La Gazelle Nero."

What we can do while we wait is honor the Games themselves, and this time we honor them in high style. I hope our stamps will be well received.

1932 Winter Olympics
Issued January 25, 1932
Lake Placid, New York

1932 Summer Olympics
Issued June 15, 1932
Los Angeles, California

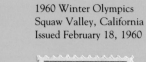

1960 Winter Olympics
Squaw Valley, California
Issued February 18, 1960

1972 Winter Olympics
Sapporo, Japan
1972 Summer Olympics
Munich, Federal Republic of Germany
Issued August 17, 1972

1976 Winter Olympics
Innsbruck, Austria
1976 Summer Olympics
Montreal, Canada
Issued July 16, 1976

1980 Winter Olympics, Lake Placid, New York
1980 Summer Olympics, Moscow, U.S.S.R.

22-cent aerogramme
Issued December 5, 1979

15-cent embossed stamped envelope
Issued December 10, 1979

31-cent international
airmail stamp
Issued November 1, 1979

10-cent domestic rate
post card stamp
Issued September 5, 1979

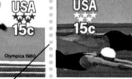
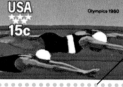

10-cent domestic rate
postal card
Issued September 17, 1979

21-cent international
airmail postal card
Issued December 1, 1979

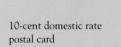
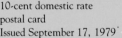

14-cent international
surface rate postal card
Issued January 15, 1980

15-cent block of four stamps
Issued September 28, 1979

15-cent block of four stamps
Issued February 1, 1980

The Art of Immortality

The artist who creates a U.S. Olympic commemorative postage stamp gets an immediate taste of immortality. The picture is quickly duplicated in quantities that would make Rembrandt gape—reproduced with a precision and fidelity brilliant enough to arouse the envy of a Hans Holbein or an Albrecht Dürer—and carried to the four corners of the earth.

Yet it was just over 50 years ago that the first U.S. Olympic stamp—a simple red two-cent denomination, showing a ski jumper (of sorts) and commemorating the Third Olympic Winter Games at Lake Placid, New York—almost didn't get issued. In October of 1931 F. A. Tilton, Third Assistant Postmaster General, wrote to Congressman Bertrand H. Snell, of New York: "It will not be practicable to provide a stamp for the event in Lake Placid in view of the fact that the Department has authorized a special stamp to commemorate the 10th Olympic Games to be held in Los Angeles next year."

Congressman Snell shot a letter to Postmaster General Walter F. Brown, protesting that he had already talked with President Hoover about the stamp. Snell enclosed a letter from Hoover himself ". . . that you may know there is no fake about this. I certainly can not understand your forgetting all of this when we had so many arguments over it. It will

be necessary to get to work on the stamp right away because it is only two months until they want it."

But were the events at Lake Placid truly "Olympic" Games? Tilton wrote Zack Farmer, General Secretary of the 10th Olympiade, to ask. Farmer assured Tilton that the winter sports at Lake Placid were "officially Olympic in every sense. . . ."

The next problem was ski jump photos. Postmaster General Brown complained to George M. Lattimer, Esq., of the Third Olympic Winter Games Committee "While these pictures are interesting . . . the figures are so small that there is practically no detail. . . ."

Lattimer suggested a different subject "—for example a ski runner or a bobsled team. We can supply you with good close-up photographs of both." And he enclosed a final ski jump photograph.

This photograph apparently did the job. On December 16th the Director of the Bureau of Engraving and Printing sent Tilton four models of the ". . . two-cent United States postage stamp, commemorating the Third Winter Olympic Games, Lake Placid, New York, for consideration." On December 29th, Postmaster General Brown announced the first U.S. commemorative for the Olympic Games.

Fifty years later, the Olympics were coming back to Los Angeles. The stamp design process had now grown almost as much as the Games. New printing techniques, more sophisticated public tastes, and a heightened appreciation of the possibilities in stamp design made the Postal Service regularly seek outside artists at the top of their profession to design commemorative stamps.

There were to be 24 stamps for the 1984 Olympics, plus three postal cards and an Olympic aerogramme. For the art, the Postal Service chose Robert Peak, an artist/illustrator who works on a grand scale. Peak had done paintings for over 130 different motion pictures: "Apocalypse Now" . . . "Camelot" . . . "My Fair Lady" . . . "Star Trek." Among his 40-odd covers for Time magazine is the sensitive and moving portrayal of Mother Teresa. His portraits of Anwar El Sadat and Thomas P. (Tip) O'Neill are in the Smithsonian collection. And Peak himself is in the "Illustrator's Hall of Fame" —an honor he shares with Stevan Dohanos, Dean of American illustrators, who served on the Postmaster General's Citizens' Stamp Advisory Committee for over 20 years, and consequently advised Peak at the outset on the Olympic assignment.

"Steve told me, 'You'll have to think small, Bob, when you're doing a stamp.' " But Peak hadn't yet realized how small. Nor did Peak anticipate the impact that the Olympic stamp assignment would have on his way of working—or his career.

"The subjects had already been selected by the Postal Service people," Peak said. "So I started on the research . . . digging through books, articles, files on athletics in general and the Olympics in particular. Selection is one of the tools you learn, in the process of creating—you don't just put things in. You have to know what you can and should leave out."

When Peak was ready to make the preliminary sketches, he met with Bradbury Thompson, a prominent book designer who would serve as art director and also arrange the lettering on the stamps. "I had to leave space for the type—and *white* space. It's no good running letters over a color."

Peak also had to make his paintings small, 7.2 by 4.2 inches—five times the size of the finished stamps—a standard the Postal Service set because larger illustrations usually had too much fine detail to print effectively.

Peak was used to working large. He tried sketching in the 7.2 by 4.2 format, to get the rhythm and a graceful weight of line. Satisfied at last that he had a workable style, Peak started on the individual sports, making several sketches for each. There was a pre-selected balance of male and female figures, and ethnic types. "I was careful to keep the uniforms entirely generic, too—no numbers, no indications of national teams."

Peak chose bands of color as an element to unify the stamp designs. "I tried to get simplicity of movement, and then group the stamps so that the individual designs worked—and yet in combinations, the angles would complement each other."

There were immediate problems. "I had trouble establishing consistency, without repeating the same design. And some subjects—particularly team sports such as volleyball—were difficult to fit into a stamp."

But Peak also found satisfactions. "There were sports objects that helped my composition—skis, barbells, a bicycle or basketball." And always, Peak sought to catch that particular instant that was the high point of the athlete's performance.

At this point, with dozens of sketches done, Peak left Scottsdale, Arizona, for Washington, D.C. At Postal Service headquarters, Peak and the experts from the Stamps Division laid out the sketches, "like a big jigsaw puzzle," and made the final selections. There were meetings with specialists from the Bureau of Engraving and Printing to arrange for printing cylinder proofs and to suggest minute art revisions that would improve printing quality. And the longest scrutiny began as each of Peak's sketches was checked for accuracy.

A commemorative stamp is seen by so many millions of people that no error—however slight—misses the eye of some expert, somewhere. The Postal Service asked the U.S. Olympic Committee to provide specialists—from college teams, coaches, Olympic competitors—who could check the accuracy of Peak's illustrations.

"The coaches objected to the long hair I showed on the woman high jumper. I'd also sketched the kayak moving over rough water—when actually, kayaking had become a smooth water Olympic event for 1984, without my realizing it."

Peak then transferred his sketches to D'Arches water color paper, and began the finished illustrations. But even as he worked, there were problems. The printing cylinder proofs made by the Bureau of Engraving and Printing had turned up color difficulties.

"I have a tendency to grey off the flesh tones a bit. When they pushed the flesh color on the press, too much red came up." Peak adjusted his scale of colors, making warmer flesh tones, careful to use cool with warm colors, "—to avoid the analogous colors, that would blend together in a stamp-sized illustration."

At last, the brightly active figures moving across the bands of color were ready to go on the 24 Olympic stamps, the three postal cards, the aerogramme. And Robert Peak had come to a realization, "—when I was about half finished, that this job was the smallest thing I'd ever done, but it would have more readership than anything else I'd ever done. That gave me a great sense of satisfaction."

For the artist, a U.S. commemorative stamp offers many satisfactions. To appear on a stamp puts a piece of art in the company of the world's master works, from the cave paintings at Altamira to the Mona Lisa. By sheer numbers, a stamp guarantees the art a form of posterity. "The bust outlasts the throne—the coin, Tiberius." And Robert Peak's vivid illustrations on the 24 Olympic stamps—printed in their millions, sent to the ends of the earth, treasured in thousands of collections—will live with the best of them.

1984 Winter Olympics, Sarajevo, Yugoslavia
1984 Summer Olympics, Los Angeles, California

30-cent aerogramme
Issued October 14, 1983

40-cent international airmail rate block of four stamps
Issued April 8, 1983

13-cent post card rate block of four stamps
Issued July 28, 1983

35-cent international airmail rate block of four stamps
Issued November 4, 1983

13-cent domestic rate postal card
Issued August 5, 1983

28-cent international rate postal card Issued December 29, 1983

13-cent postal card
Issued April 30, 1984

28-cent international airmail rate block of four stamps
Issued June 17, 1983

20-cent block of four stamps
Issued January 6, 1984

20-cent block of four stamps
Issued May 4, 1984

The Olympic Games were born from the ancient Greeks' preoccupation with individual competition, religion, respect for athletic prowess and a sense of brotherhood.

So important were these tests of physical speed, skill and strength that the first specific date of any event in Greek history is 776 BC. In that year a cook named Coroebus won the "stade," a race of approximately 200 yards, and launched a quest for athletic glory that persists today.

What began in lofty idealism and sportsmanship, however, deteriorated over the centuries into carnivals of greed and bloodshed until Roman Emperor Theodosius I abolished the Games after 392 AD.

In modern times, the Olympic Games were reborn as international competition in 1896. Despite being interrupted twice by world wars and beset by racism, national boycotts, international terrorism and runaway expenses, the Games not only endure but thrive.

While nations and athletic officials have created much of the turmoil associated with past Olympic Games, the Games remain the centerpiece of world-wide sports activity for one reason: the athletes themselves.

The Olympic story has always been filled with the high drama of individuals who conquered heartbreaks and handicaps.

The Olympic Games is Jim Thorpe, the American Indian who performed so brilliantly winning both the decathlon and pentathlon at Stockholm in 1912. Even the subsequent wrongful stripping of his gold medals could not blur the lasting imprint he made on the athletic world. He was exonerated posthumously.

It is the story of a gritty Frenchman named Joseph Guillemot who was subjected to a heavy gas attack as a World War I soldier and whose lungs were feared to be weak. Yet he entered the 5,000 meter run in 1920 and, in a stirring come-from-behind effort, edged Paavo Nurmi, the last time the Flying Finn would be beaten in a major race for years.

It is Nurmi who was forced to leave school and get odd jobs at age 12 when his father died, surviving on a vegetarian diet while living in a cramped one-room cottage. Determined to achieve distance running greatness, Peerless Paavo, in slightly more than a decade, bettered world records 35 times in distances ranging from 1,500 to 20,000 meters.

In the Olympic Games of 1920, 1924 and 1928 Nurmi won nine gold medals and three silver with an emotionless expression and effortless style. Four of the gold came at Paris in 1924, two of them within 90 minutes when he won the 1,500 meters, then beat countryman Willie Ritola by a yard at 5,000 meters. Two days later in blistering heat reaching 113 degrees, Nurmi captured the 10,000 meter cross country race that only 15 of the 39 starters could even finish.

On the eve of the 1932 Games, Nurmi was ruled ineligible when his amateur status was questioned. He was absolved 20 years later when he was given the honor of being the Olympic torch bearer at Helsinki as grateful fellow Finns stood to roar their appreciation. Despite being troubled by rheumatism Nurmi, 55, completed his lap around the stadium track in his familiar erect style. He then handed the torch to Hannes Kolehmainen, winner of four gold medals in the 1912 and 1920 Olympics and the dis-

tance runner who had been Paavo's childhood inspiration. It was, indeed, a golden moment in Olympic history.

Those same 1952 Helsinki Games were all but the private domain of a small, lean Czech army officer with thinning hair named Emil Zatopek. He won the 5,000 and 10,000 meter runs plus the first marathon he had ever attempted while his wife, Dana, captured the women's javelin event.

There was irony in the 1960 marathon because it was won by Abebe Bikila, an Ethiopian palace guard, pounding barefoot through the streets of Rome, capital city of the nation whose troops his father had battled in 1935. Four years later in Tokyo, Bikila took the taxing event again—only a month after surgery.

The Olympic story is Al Oerter, most durable of all Olympians, who won the discus throw four straight times, 1956-68. In 1964 he managed one mighty, winning throw on his last attempt in the face of searing pain from torn rib cartilage.

It is lanky Ray Ewry, confined to a wheelchair as a boy and told by doctors he might never walk again, who devised his own exercises and—beginning at age 27—won 10 gold medals over eight years in the now defunct standing high jump, long jump and triple jump.

It is Jesse Owens, grandson of a black American slave, who shattered Olympic records and the Nazi myth of racial superiority enroute to four gold medals in the sprints and long jump at the Berlin Games of 1936.

It is swimmer Mark Spitz, disappointed at his showing in 1968, who captured a record seven gold medals four years later.

It is Tennessee sprinter Wilma Rudolph, 17th of 19 children, who was motivated by childhood illnesses including scarlet fever, rheumatic fever and polio which left her crippled and scorned by other kids. "The only thing I ever really wanted was to be normal," she recalls. Wilma won three titles at Rome.

It is a 30-year old Dutch housewife and mother of two, named Fanny Blankers-Koen, winning four sprints and hurdles events in the face of mounting emotional fatigue at London in 1948. It is Norwegian figure skater Sonja Henie dominating three Winter Games, Russian speedskater Lydia Skoblikova winning six gold medals and Australian swimmer Dawn Fraser capturing eight medals despite bronchial asthma.

Olympic golden moments include Bob Mathias at age 17, a boyhood victim of anemia, winning the first of two titles in the gruelling decathlon and blazing a trail for fellow American decathletes Rafer Johnson, Bill Toomey and Bruce Jenner.

There was the favored 1956 Yale eight-oared crew, finishing a beaten third in its first heat but saved by the Olympic repechage (second chance) system, winning three rugged races in as many days over 2,000 meters to bring home the gold.

And Americans will long remember a young, relatively inexperienced but enthusiastic hockey team which beat the Russian nationals—rated by many experts the finest in the world including professionals—enroute to a gold medal in 1980.

Olympic champions also include swimmer Johnny Weismuller, considered a weakling in infancy, who later played "Tarzan" in films; high jumper Walt Davis, who had had polio; weightlifter Paul Anderson who had a kidney ailment, and Hungarian rapid fire pistol ace Karoly Takacs. The latter lost his shooting hand in a grenade explosion—so he became left-handed and won the gold in 1948 and 1952.

Dedication is personified by Harrison (Bones) Dillard who failed to qualify in his high hurdles specialty in 1948, barely made it in the 100 meter sprints and was the upset winner in that event. He returned in '52 to capture the hurdles.

The Olympics is Marine Lt. Billy Mills, who originally began running to get in shape for boxing while attending an Indian school for orphans, rallying from 10 yards back with 100 to go to win the 10,000 meters in 1964, America's first distance gold medal since 1908. He had run the distance only five times before and never had won a big race. It is Austrian farmhand Leonhard Stock, named to the team only 24 hours earlier, winning a downhill ski race for the first time in his life for the 1980 gold medal. The victory came only two months after he broke his left collarbone.

On the succeeding pages are a series of Olympic golden moments in sports depicted in the U.S. Postal Service's 1983-84 Olympic commemorative issues of stamps, postal cards and an aerogramme.

Even a man with extraordinary strength, a zest for living and a wife named Olimpiada can suddenly find himself an underdog in the sport he has dominated. It happened to Soviet super-heavyweight weightlifter Vasily Alexeyev in Montreal.

His response to the challenge provided another golden moment in the annals of the Olympic Games.

To hundreds of millions of television viewers during two Olympics it was apparent this son of a Russian lumberjack born in the tiny village of Pokrovo-Shishking was no ordinary muscleman.

Alexeyev had a sense of humor, a sense of the theatrical and the instinct to 'psyche' rivals. He believed in hard work but geared to his highly individual plan—practicing sometimes at 2 or 3 a.m. and serving as his own coach for a long period of time.

And when the 6-foot-2, 345-pounder wasn't shattering 80 world records during his weightlifting career, he was mastering the subtle shots of table tennis, the timing of volleyball and the delicate sauces vital to the art of an amateur chef.

Despite a back ailment, this lover of roses and his own singing won his first world title in 1970. During that meet he became the first man to lift 500 pounds (501.5) in the clean and jerk, his best event.

By the time he arrived at the '72 Munich Games, Alexeyev was the dominant figure in his class. First

Belgium's Serge Reding in the press, then America's Ken Patera in the snatch were so intimidated each started his lifts at too high a weight and each failed in three tries.

Alexeyev finished with a three-lift total of 1,410.95 pounds to 1,344.8 for the Federal Republic of Germany's Rudolph Mang with Gerd Bonk of the German Democratic Republic winning the bronze medal.

Four years later at Montreal, the 34-year-old mining engineer was no longer the favorite. Bonk and Bulgaria's Khristo Plachkov, 10 and 11 years his junior, respectively, had surpassed his records in the clean and jerk and in total weight lifted.

Undismayed by circumstances, Alexeyev had lost none of his strength, competitiveness and supreme confidence. Injury and illness caused Plachkov to withdraw in embarrassment.

In between practice sessions, the winner of Russia's coveted Order of Lenin, calmly went fishing.

At the showdown, Bonk lifted 375 pounds in the snatch while Alexeyev waited in a nearby room. The press event had been dropped from the competition. Alexeyev then appeared, started at 386 pounds and on his final try lifted 408.

Bonk still had a chance in the clean and jerk but his best was 517½ pounds.

Alexeyev earlier had lifted 507, his previous Olympic record, which assured him of his second straight gold medal. But he wanted to be first in the event, too. He ordered weights added for a try at a world record 561¾ pounds.

Amid cheers he slowly approached the bar, closed his eyes, bellowed, lifted the bar to his shoulders, then over his head, staggered under the massive weight, then stood still—and victorious. He had lifted 969¾ pounds in two events to Bonk's 892½. Mission accomplished!

Between 1970 and 1977, Vasily Alexeyev never lost a weightlifting competition.

What do parking lots, honey, yoga, hypnosis and African tribal chants have in common? They are all elements in the path Parry O'Brien traveled to two Olympic gold medals in the shot-put.

The California individualist never overlooked any possibility that would give him a competitive edge. But the cornerstones of his success were hard work, development of an unorthodox style to fit his needs, a weight program and mental preparation.

By the fall of 1951 as a 6-foot-3, 220 pound sophomore at the University of Southern California, O'Brien made two pivotal decisions. First, he gave up football, in which he had starred as a freshman halfback and end, to concentrate on the shot-put. Second, he had thought about a new method of throwing the iron ball and decided to go all-out with the technique in his preparations for the 1952 season.

Previously, shot-putters had started at the back of the throwing ring, arched their bodies to help propel the 16-pound object, skipped across the circle and pushed the ball forward. Later, athletes began standing sideways to the throwing lane, then spinning 90 degrees to throw.

Enter O'Brien, judged not to have great natural ability but possessing unusual speed for his size.

In the spring of '51, he had won his first major event, the national A.A.U. championship with a toss of 55 feet, 9¼ inches. But he concluded that using the old style he could never do better than 56 feet—and he had visions of achieving the impossible dream of the field events: a 60-foot throw.

O'Brien turned his back to the throwing area and spun a full 180 degrees, giving him more distance in which to build up speed and power behind the throw which he rolled off his fingers.

O'Brien spent countless hours, when he wasn't at the track, practicing in the parking lot behind his fraternity house to sharpen his skills, sometimes needing a flashlight to find the iron ball. The man who coached himself and said he always liked being a "soloist," turned in as many as 150 practice throws a day—until his hands bled.

The payoffs in 1952 were N.C.A.A. and A.A.U. titles prior to the Olympic Trials in which his 57-½ throw was second to that of his arch-rival, Darrow Hooper, at 57-1⅜.

Under ominous skies at the '52 Helsinki Games, O'Brien calculated he needed to put everything into his first attempt to beat the rain. He got an Olympic record 57-1½, then barely held on to stave off Hooper, winning the gold by ¾ of an inch.

For years to come, O'Brien was to be a dominant figure in the shot-put, drinking honey for quick energy, studying yoga and self-hypnosis to help him achieve greater powers of concentration and listening to unusual music, such as tribal chants, to pitch himself very high for competition.

Using a weight training program to fullest advantage, O'Brien kept up his blitz, setting a world record of 59-¾ in 1953. It was on May 8, 1954, two days after Dr. Roger Bannister became the first man in history to run a mile in under four minutes, that Parry realized his goal of being the first 60 foot shot-putter. The toss was 60-5¼. Ironically it was another May 8—1965—when Randy Matson broke the 70-foot barrier (70-7) in a meet at Texas A.&M.

Admittedly nervous at the 1956 Melbourne Games, O'Brien managed 60-11¼, well below the 63-2 he had just accomplished in a Los Angeles meet. But all five of his Olympic tries were better than the best of his competition so Parry had another gold medal.

By 1960, at the age of 28, O'Brien was not improving in the face of younger, bigger, stronger rivals. Nevertheless he took the early Olympic lead in Rome. Only countryman Bill Neider's final toss of 64-6¾ caused him to settle for a silver medal at 62-8½.

Parry gave it one more try at the 1964 Tokyo Games and although his 63-0 effort was his best ever in Olympic competition he could do no better than fourth.

O'Brien didn't quit until age 34 in 1966 after achieving his personal best throw of 64-7½. During his most productive years he was also ranked high in the discus throw and, in 1957, was No. 1 in the world in that event.

The United States won 14 gold medals in the shot-put through 1968 led by O'Brien, Neider, Dallas Long and Matson.

Russia's Vladimir Kiselyov authored the first 70-foot Olympic throw, 70-½, at Moscow in 1980.

While winning three Olympic medals, shot-putter Parry O'Brien added more than four feet to the world record during his career.

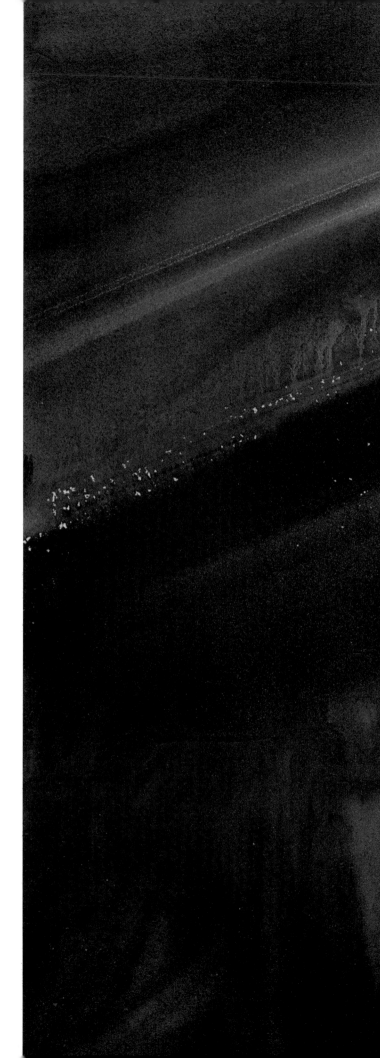

Russian Nikolai Andrianov edged Japan's Sawao Kato by one point for the all-around championship in the 1976 Montreal Olympics. The moment signalled a transition of supremacy between two superb athletes and a change in the balance of power in a comparatively unrecognized sport—men's gymnastics.

Precision, skill, strength and daring are necessary ingredients to achieving prominence in gymnastics. Yet it took a combination of world-wide television and dramatically graceful female performances in the 1972 and 1976 Games to focus public attention on the sport.

The men's competition remained a step-child to women's events from the spectators' viewpoint.

Too bad. Kato and Andrianov were masters.

At the age of 19, Andrianov burst upon the Olympic scene with boyish enthusiasm at Munich in 1972, winning a gold medal in the floor exercise by 5/100ths of a point over Japan's Akinori Nakayama. Meanwhile Kato, a physical education student who was six years older than Andrianov, won his second straight individual all-around Olympic crown despite shoulder and lumbar disc injuries.

Japanese coach Yukio Endo, 1964 Olympic all-around king at Tokyo, had predicted a sweep of all eight men's gold medals at Munich, but his athletes fell three short. In their efforts to prove superior talent, the Japanese risked more difficult exercises. The Russians generally played it safer, exhibiting technical excellence. But Andrianov tackled tougher programs.

The 5-foot-7, 143-pound Andrianov first drew attention to his skill when he went to the 1970 world championships as a reserve team member. Mikhail Voronin, the favorite an unheralded Kato had upset for the '68 Olympic all-around title, said of Andrianov: "He does everything uninhibitedly, almost playfully, and brings the beauty of gymnastics to the spectator with true artistic grace."

In Montreal, a far more confident, mature, disciplined Andrianov captured gold medals in the floor exercise and on the rings and vault as well as besting Kato in the all-around competition.

Out of seven individual gold medals, Andrianov had won four to two for Japan, one of them by Kato on the parallel bars. The tide was turning. Yet Kato, coming out of semi-retirement, still helped Japan win its fifth consecutive Olympic team title dating from 1960.

At the 1980 Moscow Games, Andrianov won a gold medal in the vault, a silver in the all-around and aided the Soviets in recapturing the men's team crown they took in their first Olympic participation in 1952 and retained in 1956.

Married to an Olympic gold medal winning gymnast, Lyubov Burda, the snub-nosed Andrianov traveled a very bumpy road to success from the old Russian town of Vladimir. As a kid he was difficult, disobedient, fought with the girls at recess and sometimes skipped school to relax by the river.

One day a friend dragged him to a gym where the instructor wrote in his diary: "Enrolled Nikolai Andrianov. Abilities average. Obstinate."

Later, Andrianov tried to quit his gymnastics course but Instructor Tolkachov refused to take no for an answer. With patience and understanding, Nikolai caught the competitive fever, trained hard and sought ever-tougher exercises.

In three Olympics Andrianov wound up with seven gold, four silver and two bronze medals; captaincy of the Russian national team and the prized Order of Lenin decoration.

The 118-pound Kato captured eight gold and three silver medals plus one bronze in the Olympics covering the span of 1968-76.

The most successful and consistent Olympic male gymnast, 1972-80, was Russia's Nikolai Andrianov.

America's terrific teenagers were primed to cap the dramatic 1960s resurgence of U.S. women's swimming at the Mexico City Olympic Games. Deborah Elizabeth Meyer, central figure in the plot, had been named 1967 Woman Athlete of the Year by the Soviet news agency, Tass.

The 16-year-old from Sacramento, California, was the pre-Olympic favorite to capture three gold medals.

When the blond schoolgirl showed up at the Olympic Village hobbling with a crutch under her right arm, a momentary shudder went through the ranks of America's Water Babies. Later, at a vital point in the competition, Meyer was so sick from a sore throat and an intestinal ailment it was feared she would be unable to continue.

But Debbie Meyer did not reach the top of the swimming world by being a quitter.

To better understand the 1968 Mexico City setting, keep in mind American women swimmers won 10 individual Olympic gold medals in the period 1912-1932. But in the war-interrupted 1936-56 span they managed only two golds in four Olympiads.

At that point, the United States fostered a national age-group swimming program. The specialized training and regular competition produced more and better prepared swimmers—and three gold medals each in women's individual events at both Rome and Tokyo.

So when the U.S. girls headed south of the border in 1968 it was for gold prospecting. With the help of added events they brought back 11 gold medals, eight individual and three relay firsts.

Working hard at the sport she loved but not making much progress, a hopeful Debbie Meyer watched the 1964 Olympics on television. As incentive, her father gave her a stopwatch inscribed: "Mexico City, 1968." The following year he got a job transfer from New Jersey to California for Debbie's asthma and swimming future.

She was soon under the demanding direction of swimming coach Sherman Chavoor who insisted distance and endurance were prerequisites for freestyle swimmers. Debbie remembers the first time she practiced for him. Chavoor told her to warm up with 20 laps and "I couldn't even do four."

Two years later she was winning races and international admiration consistently.

Just before leaving for Mexico City, Debbie turned an ankle. But for her initial workout at the Olympic complex she threw away the crutch.

The first time she entered the water in a trial heat, Meyer shattered the Olympic record for the 400 meter freestyle in 4:35, then lowered it to 4:31.8 Sunday leading the entire final race.

By the next morning she had a sore throat, a stomach infection and penicillin to try to fight off both. Ahead were the 800 meter heat and 200 meter final.

Tired but determined she showed up for the Tuesday afternoon heat shivering, wrapped in a blanket and unwilling to take medication for her stomach pains for fear it might contain a drug which could disqualify her. Debbie reached within herself and did another Chavoor endurance drill—with high stakes. She coasted to a 9:48.8 time in the 800 trial, winning by 25 meters.

By far her toughest test would be the 200 meter final at night. She tried to concentrate on swimming and forget the pain. As usual, Meyer got a fast start but instead of pulling away felt some of her strength ebb and by the second of the four laps U.S. teammate Jan Henne began closing. The two matched stroke for stroke on the final pool length until Debbie mustered one last burst to out-touch her rival. It was an Olympic record 2:10.5.

Two days later, feeling no ill effects, Meyer easily outdistanced seven other competitors in the 800 meter final. She thus became the first woman swimmer to win three individual gold medals in one Olympic Games.

Including relay events American women have won 89 gold medals in swimming compared to 34 in track and field going into the 1984 Games.

Other Olympic women swimming greats include Australian Dawn Fraser, 1956-64, who won four gold and four silver medals and the German Democratic Republic's Kornelia Ender, 1972-76, four gold and five silver. At 27 in Tokyo, 'Granny' Fraser won her third consecutive 100 meter crown only half a year after she received chipped neck vertebrae in an auto accident in which her mother was killed.

In men's competition the honor roll is headed by Americans Mark Spitz, Don Schollander, John Naber, Johnny Weissmuller, Duke Kahanamoku and John Hencken; Australian Murray Rose and East German Roland Matthes.

Spitz won 11 medals including seven gold and seven world records in 1972 at Munich. Weissmuller, who never lost a freestyle race in a decade of competition, won five swimming gold medals, 1924-28, and added a bronze in water polo.

Freestyle swimmer Debbie Meyer would not be denied three gold medals at the 1968 Mexico City Games.

For lack of a shoe, Ferenc Puskas developed the deadliest left foot in soccer. He was the short, chubby, unlikely-looking catalyst who helped make Hungary's "Magic Magyars" the best team in Olympic history.

Puskas grew up on the dusty streets of Kispest, a Budapest suburb, the second son of a mediocre soccer player. His toy was a ball made of rags and old socks.

Nicknamed "Ocsi" (kid brother), Puskas said his father could only afford one pair of shoes for the two boys and he always wore the right one. Because he couldn't risk damaging the precious shoe, Puskas maintained that his shoeless left foot practicing led to a powerful, accurate shot.

Even after he had reached international stardom, Puskas continued to hone his skills in endless drills of kicking a ball against a brick wall and using his body to manipulate the rebound.

Under the post-World War II communist administration, Hungarian soccer was revamped by the founding of the Honved army club in 1948. It absorbed Puskas' Kispest team and had the pick of the nation's top players.

Ostensibly in military training, the playful, brash and skilled Puskas had a singular army detail as did his teammates: play soccer.

Inside left Puskas, now the "Galloping Major," was paired with acrobatic inside right Sandor Kocsis whose shooting prowess with the top of his anatomy earned him the title "Golden Head." Both were awesome scorers.

The last line of defense was a superb goaltender, Gyula Grosics, who constantly shouted directions and encouragement to his teammates, frequently ventured out of the penalty area and occasionally was labeled a "fourth back."

Entering the 1952 Helsinki Olympics, Hungary fielded a disciplined, precise and innovative "side." Coach Gustav Sebes had developed a forward line alignment resembling the letter "W" with center forward Nandor Hidegkuti playing well back of Puskas and Kocsis, mainly to feed passes to the freelancing stars.

After a rugged 2-1 victory over Romania in which 48 free kicks were awarded due to rough play, Hungary breezed past Italy 3-0, Turkey 7-1 and Sweden 6-0 into the final. Yugoslavia had been held to a 5-5 overtime draw by Russia but won the rematch 3-1 enroute to the title game.

A crowd of 50,000 saw Hungary win the gold medal, 2-0, in a contest if not dramatic certainly a technical masterpiece. Puskas, injured in the first half when he missed a penalty kick, feinted a defender into falling down before driving home a goal after intermission. Later, his perfect kick landed at the feet of outside left Zoltan Czibor who split the Yugoslavians with a shot that scored.

One year later the Hungarian team stunned England 6-3 at Wembley Stadium—the first foreign international team ever to win on British soil—and then proved its superiority 7-1 in a Budapest rematch.

Between May 1950 and February 1956, the "Magic Magyars" lost only one of 48 matches. That came in the 1954 World Cup final, a stunning 3-2 setback to West Germany after Hungary took an early 2-0 lead. Puskas played badly hurt.

Hungary has won three Olympic soccer medals, adding 1964 and 1968 to 1952's brilliant showing. The team was upset by Poland, 2-1, in the 1972 final and took a bronze medal in 1960.

Hungarian soccer team (in white) during its 2-0 win over Yugoslavia in the final 1952 match at Helsinki.

This is the story of Moses, logic and The Lord.

When he reached his 19th birthday in 1975, Edwin Corley Moses was an honor student physics major at Morehouse College in Atlanta. The long-legged offspring of two public school officials in Dayton, Ohio, was also a multi-talented athlete.

What Moses wanted was to compete in the Olympic Games the following year. He had come to Morehouse as a budding quarter mile runner who also dabbled in the high hurdles.

Edwin's parents had always stressed to him the importance of a good education, the value of careful thinking and the pride which goads a man to do his best in anything he attempts.

After poring over the list of track and field candidates, Moses reasoned the established athletes in the 400 meter run and 110 meter hurdles were too good. Logic told him if he wanted to make the U.S. team he would have to pick another event. It led him to settle on the 400 meter or intermediate hurdles, a combination of the other two events.

Just one problem. By the end of 1975 Moses had reluctantly run that particular event only once in his life and his time, by his own admission, was very forgettable.

With his analytical mind, Edwin began to chart his Olympic 'Mission: Montreal.' The intermediate hurdles involves 10 hurdles, each 36 inches high, spaced 35 meters apart. It requires full-throttle speed, endurance for the distance and strategic timing to clear the barriers cleanly and in stride.

Earlier, Edwin had been an all-star Little League baseball catcher, a basketball guard who could dunk the ball when he was only 5-feet-8 and a defensive back in football. But he preferred track where he had to rely only on himself.

On his Olympic campaign, Moses taught himself to run the intermediate hurdles. Rev. Lloyd Jackson, minister of the African Methodist Episcopal Church, was his unpaid 'coach' helping him with his mental outlook. Edwin handled the rest.

For the strength and endurance he needed to maintain speed and form over the last three hurdles, Moses trained by running cross country. He later explained: "Runners start to lose it on the sixth hurdle. The first five are nothing, really, because you're not fatigued yet. The far turn is the Twilight Zone."

For the flexibility he wanted to achieve, Moses turned his hand to ballet, yoga and martial arts exercises.

His plan was very precise—six weeks of intensive practice.

On March 27, 1976, Moses won the Florida Relays in 50.1 seconds, thus qualifying for the Olympic Trials in only his second 400-meter hurdles competition. A mere four months and six meets later, this relatively unknown running machine stunned the track world by winning an Olympic gold medal in the world record time of :47.64.

Because his nation decided to boycott the Games, defending champion John Akii-Bua of Uganda was not in Montreal. Moses was confident he was well prepared. He won his semifinal heat in an American record time of :48.29, then took a four-hour nap before the final.

Wearing tinted prescription glasses and a wristwatch accurate to hundredths of a second, Moses got a terrific start in the showdown race as did the Soviet Union's Yevgeniy Gavrilyenko and Mike Shine of Penn State. Moses and Gavrilyenko reached the curve in front with Shine close behind.

But at the seventh hurdle Edwin pulled away and won the race by eight meters over Shine with the Russian finishing third.

Afterward Rev. Jackson said Moses prayed with him before every race.

"We ask The Lord to bless us, to help Edwin, to give him guidance and strength and whatever he needs," he said. "I guess The Lord has been smiling with him all the way."

Yet the 6-foot-1, 160 pound perfectionist felt he had lost at least .8 of a second in mistakes and called his gold medal performance "real raggedy."

"My arms came away from my sides, some of my leg follow-throughs were bad," Moses reflected. "I'm still learning this race."

While Glenn Davis won two gold medals in the intermediate hurdles, Olympic history in the 110-meter event is dotted with American victors like Harrison (Bones) Dillard, Lee Calhoun, Willie Davenport and Alvin Kraenzlein.

In women's hurdles, the outstanding performers include Mildred (Babe) Didrikson Zaharias, later of professional golfing fame, Dutch housewife Fanny Blankers-Koen and Australia's Shirley de la Hunty.

At the 1976 Olympics, Edwin Moses (top) was the only world-class hurdler who could maintain 13 strides between each hurdle throughout the race.

"On the uneven bars, she whirls as easily as a sparrow fluttering from limb to limb on a tree. On the balance beam she clings to it as surely as a squirrel would. On the vault, she lands as softly as a sea gull on a beach. In her floor exercises, she is part go-go dancer, part ballerina, part cheerleader."

The words are those of New York Times sports columnist Dave Anderson. They describe a Romanian schoolgirl named Nadia Comaneci who, athletically, gave new meaning to the phrase "Perfect 10."

For three summer days in 1976 the Montreal Forum rocked from volleys of tumultuous shouting and standing ovations. It sounded like Les Canadiens had again won hockey's coveted Stanley Cup, but the attention was not on burly men with skates and sticks.

Instead, the spotlight was on a tiny princess of precision who was revolutionizing women's gymnastics while momentarily unifying a troubled world in breathless admiration. Nadia, an 86 pound, 14-year old collector of dolls, seven times was awarded unprecedented perfect 10 Olympic scores.

She so captivated her elders that many paid scalpers as much as $200. for a $16. ticket to watch the daughter of a factory mechanic make history.

Four years earlier in Munich the world had cried and laughed with Olga Korbut, the endearing Soviet sprite. Although not very expressive, Comaneci inspired awe for her superb technique. As Anderson wrote, "she's so good you get a chill watching her."

Together the two child prodigies brought a focus on and appreciation for the demanding yet artistic sport it had never before enjoyed.

Displaying daring, courage and style in her difficult routines, Comaneci achieved four '10's on the uneven bars and three more on the four-inch-wide balance beam. She won gold medals in those events and in the combined exercises.

It took two more '10's by Russia's Nelli Kim to edge teammate Ludmila Turischeva for the gold in the horse vault and floor exercise.

Accidentally discovered by Romanian coach Bela Karolyi when she was a kindergarten student, Nadia wowed the Olympic crowd with her floor exercise program done to the tune "Yes Sir, That's My Baby." That won her a bronze medal and she collected a silver in team combined exercises.

Comaneci was to win two more gold medals in the 1980 Moscow Olympics.

But the high drama was in Montreal. The girl with the pigtails and wiggle from the mountain town of Onesti was thrust into an impressive field. She was more than up to the challenge.

Korbut, now 21 and a sentimental favorite, won a silver medal in the beam amid cries of "C'mon Olga." A touching moment came when Turischeva, who won nine medals including four gold 1968-76, kissed Nadia on the victory stand.

When it was over, Comaneci said: "I knew all along if I persevered, I just might make it. This represented to me a lot of my hard work."

"I think she's the best gymnast the world has ever known," commented Frank Burke, Executive Director of the U.S. Gymnastics Federation.

The dignified Turischeva was stepping down after an illustrious career and a year later married sprint champion Valeri Borzov.

A list of previous greats in women's gymnastics starts with Russia's Larisa Latynina, mother of two, and converted ice skater Vera Caslavska of Czechoslovakia, who met in many memorable competitions.

Gymnast Nadia Comaneci, a little girl with a big talent, stole the show at the 1976 Montreal Olympics.

United States supremacy in Olympic basketball struggled out of the Berlin mud to reach a golden climax in Mexico City on the efforts of a belittled team of also-rans.

The 1968 winners acted out a real-life fairy tale.

Since basketball became a part of the official Olympic program in 1936, U.S. teams had not lost a single contest in six Summer Games. But the Mexican setting was different.

Other nations were improving so rapidly in the sport that some arrived bigger, stronger—and at least a few, reportedly, better—than the Americans. The list of players who did not try out for the U.S. squad, lured by professional contracts and a black athletes' protest movement, read like a "Who's Who": Lou Alcindor (later Kareem Abdul Jabbar), Elvin Hayes, Wes Unseld, Bob Lanier.

Venerable Hank Iba, 64, coach of these first-ever Yankee underdogs, knew that to have any chance he would have to stress defense and team play to a group of young men practicing together just a few short weeks versus national squads playing as units for four years.

His raw material included a relatively unknown 19-year old center, Spencer Haywood, his tallest starter as a 6-foot-8 center from Trinidad Junior College and Detroit; guard Jo Jo White of Kansas; Mike Silliman, 24-year old army captain from Louisville; little Charlie Scott, North Carolina, and a rubber company foreman, Calvin Fowler, 28, of Akron, Ohio.

In its fourth game, the U.S. whipped powerful Yugoslavia 73-58 as White excelled with 24 points

and outstanding playmaking. Iba's Cinderella kids swept into the semifinals, defeating Brazil 74-63 while Yugoslavia stunned the gold medal favorite, Russia, 63-62.

That set up a U.S.-Yugoslav final that stood a tense 32-29 at halftime. Then the Americans applied a full-court press defense, scored 17 straight points at the start of the second half and pulled away to a 65-50 triumph. Haywood, under doctor's care for a severe case of diarrhea, scored 23 points, grabbed 10 rebounds, blocked five shots and held Yugoslavian high scorer Dragutin Cermak to five points while he was guarding him.

White, who added 14 points and superb floor play, commented on the team's prideful reaction to predictions that it had virtually no chance to sweep through unbeaten to another gold medal: "When people underrate you, that's when you have to bear down. I thought everybody underrated this team."

Added Iba: "When given the chance and when properly handled, the American athlete can do just about anything. I think we proved that."

If 1968 was the rags-to-riches team, the 1960 U.S. entry was perhaps the most awesome because in eight games it averaged 102 points and a 42.4 point winning margin. Oscar Robertson and Jerry West went on to be the all-time star guards in the professional National Basketball Association where teammates Jerry Lucas, Walt Bellamy, Terry Dischinger, Bob Boozer, Adrian Smith and Darrell Imhoff also were to become headline performers.

A close rival was the 1956 squad powered by 6-foot-9 Bill Russell and 6-1 K. C. Jones who had just led San Francisco to two straight national collegiate championships and a 55-game winning streak. The defensively-supreme U.S. team romped through eight games—beating the Russians twice,

85-55 in the preliminary round and 89-55 in the final. Russell did not permit Russia's 7-4, 340 pound Ivan Krouminch a single field goal in the title game.

Invented by Dr. James Naismith, a teacher of psychology, Bible study and boxing at the time at the Springfield, Massachusetts Y.M.C.A. Training School, basketball got off to a shaky Olympic start in 1936 at Berlin. Baffled by the sport, the Germans built the courts outdoors on a red clay surface and saw their team lose one of its games, 20-0, to Czechoslovakia.

Dr. Naismith threw up the first ball in the opening game between Japan and China, already at war. The first game opponent for the U.S.—Spain—did not appear due to a civil war. The Americans had to wear makeshift outfits in the quarterfinals when their lockers were burglarized.

The court was swept by wind and rain and was under an inch of water in the final, won by the U.S. 19-8 over Canada. One American player started to dribble downcourt and the ball stuck in the mud, as 6-foot-7 Joe Fortenberry scored 8 points and caught two wind-blown Canadian shots.

Luckily for the U.S., the International Olympic Committee did not sanction a proposal, sponsored by Japan and Mexico, that no player as tall as 6-3 be permitted to compete in Olympic basketball.

In 1964, Bill Bradley, only American Olympian ever to be named a Rhodes Scholar and win a U.S. Senate seat, was the playmaker in a Tokyo sweep.

Eight years later the American record of never having lost a single Olympics game was shattered by the Soviet Union, 51-50.

Dating from 1936, the United States men's basketball teams won 62 consecutive Olympic games until the 1972 finale in Munich, marred by an official's error.

Boxing's "big men" traditionally draw public attention. Muhammad Ali, Joe Frazier, George Foreman and Floyd Patterson moved on to fame, fortune and professional world heavyweight championships after winning Olympic gold medals.

Doggedly determined Ray Charles (Sugar Ray) Leonard, a light welterweight yet, overcame this size fixation, sharp pain in both hands and a formidable foe to become the darling of the entire athletic world in 1976.

Extremely personable and attractive, the 20-year-old from Palmer Park, Maryland, arrived in Montreal as America's best bet for a gold medal. Coach Pat Nappi, who molded the U.S. boxing team into a family-type unit which worked and prayed together, called Leonard "a boxer-puncher who is a real classy fighter."

Leonard had the quick, mobile, active style well suited for the Olympics. There are five judges in major international amateur competition (the referee has no vote) looking for the number rather than severity of blows delivered and a boxer's finesse in trying to fend off the opponent.

On the other hand, the good-looking, clean-cut charmer was an enigma to rivals who found he was faster and could both administer and absorb more punishment than they thought.

Four years earlier, Leonard had lied about his age—he was 16 and the minimum age was 17—in an unsuccessful attempt to make the Olympic team. Now, after resisting the temptation to turn professional despite his financially poor status, Sugar Ray had a problem.

The knuckles on his right hand had been painfully swollen from the start. All the way to the final Leonard had fought virtually one-handed, relying

34

on lightning left jabs and hooks. Also utilizing agility, great lateral footwork and the ability to out-think opponents, Sugar Ray moved past the likes of Britain's Clinton McKenzie, Ulrich Beyer of East Germany and Kazimier Szczerba of Poland to within three rounds of his golden goal.

En route Leonard had suffered an injury to the outside of his left hand, making it difficult to form a tight fist. Determined to go all-out despite his personal double jeopardy, Sugar Ray had to have both hands iced before the championship bout, then slipped a picture of his girl friend, Juanita, in his shoe for good luck.

His opponent was Andres Aldama, a hard-hitting, aggressive, unorthodox southpaw member of the powerful Cuban team. Aldama had hit Bulgaria's Vladimir Kolev so hard in a semi-final match that the loser was carried unconscious on a stretcher from the ring.

Sore hands and all, Leonard stuck with the battle plan: Abandon some of the cleverness which had drawn shouts of 'Ali' in his earlier fights and concentrate on hitting hard from in close.

"He's tough," Leonard said later. "I didn't want him connecting with any of those roundhouse lefts."

Moving rapidly and unleashing furious punches in combination, he began to wear down the Cuban, flooring him near the end of the second round. In the third, Sugar Ray pounded Aldama into a wobbly target by the finish for a unanimous decision.

"This is my last fight. My dream is fulfilled," Leonard said. Later, nearly penniless and confronted by the illness of both parents, he returned to the ring and won the world welterweight title.

In the 1976 Olympics, Sugar Ray Leonard helped the U.S. boxing team win 35 of 41 bouts and five gold medals.

Dick Fosbury was a very unlikely candidate for an Olympic championship in 1968. After all, he seemed to be doing everything backward.

What's more, he was hurting, nervous and talking to himself.

For generations, the world had recognized the two most common styles of high jumping as the western roll and straddle jump. In both, the jumper takes off with the forward foot and the body passes over the bar parallel to it.

When Richard D. Fosbury first started high jumping in fifth grade in Medford, Oregon, he used the straddle style and cleared 3 feet, 10 inches. By the time he was in high school he had struggled to just 5 feet, 4 inches.

Fosbury figured he wasn't improving enough because the traditional style was too complicated. He felt he could do better by going over the bar backward, thus lowering the center of gravity.

What resulted was a revolutionary new technique later to be known as the "Fosbury Flop."

Fosbury explained: "I take off on my right, or outside, foot, rather than my left foot. Then I turn my back to the bar, arch my back over the bar (head first) and then kick my legs out to clear the bar."

Despite the adverse reaction of many coaches, Fosbury soon was jumping at 5-10. When he entered Oregon State as a civil engineering major in 1965, Fosbury was told by coach Berny Wagner to go back to the more conventional style. But the conversion was short-lived.

Entering the 1968 indoor season, Fosbury as a 6-foot-4 junior was primed. Armed with the "flop," a burning desire to win and a tendency to gain more than the usual inspiration from crowd reaction, he cleared seven feet or better five times. The climax was his best ever, 7-1½, for the NCAA indoor title.

The innovative blond's momentum catapulted him through the outdoor campaign to another NCAA championship at 7-2¼ and into the Mexico City-like altitude of Lake Tahoe for the Olympic trials. He needed all three tries to clear 7-2 but on his first attempt he registered his own best-ever when the bar was placed at 7-3.

If the "flop" had a drawback it was in the landing. The point of contact was the shoulder blades or neck. Although a trained gymnast, Fosbury admitted worrying about possible injury.

"Sometimes I see movies, and really wonder how I do it," he confessed.

There was considerable wonder among the spectators in Mexico City the day of the Olympic qualifying round when Fosbury took on an impressive field including 14 other athletes who had jumped 7 feet or better. Fosbury was so psyched up he made good on his first try at each height to qualify easily.

The next day was the showdown Fosbury had been building toward. There were obstacles in addition to the dozen other finalists. "I have a bad back and I lost a big patch of skin on the back of my left heel," he said later. "Then I tripped on some stone steps the other day and strained a ligament in my right foot."

While the capacity crowd of 80,000 reacted to the unorthodox style in noisy admiration and disbelief, Fosbury fidgeted, meditated, took his time.

He cleared 6-8, 6-10¼, then 7¼, Russia's V. Gavrilov passing his turn at the latter height. Time and tension mounted.

A nervous jumper with a white shoe on his right foot and blue shoe on the left, Fosbury would rock back and forth while standing at the start of the runway, clenching and unclenching his fists for what seemed an eternity.

"I have to psych myself up," he explained. "It's concentration. I tell myself 'Go over the bar.' It's positive thinking convincing myself that I'll make it."

Gavrilov, America's Edward Carruthers and Fosbury each made 7-2⅝. At 7-3⅜ the intense Oregonian and his country man succeeded, the tiring Russian did not.

The next height was 7-4¼. Carruthers narrowly missed, Fosbury failed twice but he upped his concentration level even more and hurled his body up and over on his last chance. He leaped out of the pit his arms held high in victory.

"Every time I approach the bar I keep telling myself 'I can do it, I can do it,' " Fosbury said afterward, adding he was "mentally and physically weary."

Olympic coach Payton Jordan said of 1968 high jump gold medalist Dick Fosbury: "I've never seen anybody else ever jump that way. Fosbury is absolutely amazing."

If you liked Cinderella, you would have loved Luann Ryon.

She took up archery in 1972 because she needed a physical education course at Riverside City College in California. Her first instructor was a bowling coach. Yet four years later Luann was an Olympic champion.

In fiction, the bow and arrow are associated with Apollo, Cupid, Robin Hood, William Tell, Hiawatha. Historically, Egypt once upset Persia with the weapon, England outlasted France in the 100 Years War because of superior archers and Benjamin Franklin once suggested to the Continental Army that bows and arrows are "good weapons not wisely laid aside."

In athletics, archery was added to the official Olympic Games program when 95 competitors from 27 countries met at Munich in 1972. Americans Doreen Wilber and John Williams were the big winners.

Meanwhile for her course requirements Luann from Parker Dam, California, chose archery because she liked the challenge of target shooting. Her hobbies included darts, music and reading.

Although her first coach, Sonia Doshna, was not knowledgeable on archery's fine points at the time, according to Luann, she did heighten Ryon's interest in the sport. Later Lois Cresgy coached her at the college.

In four years of collegiate competition she kept in the running but never won anything until 1976.

With the Olympic gold medalist Williams now giving his guidance, Ryon captured a few tournaments including the California State Championship.

Still, she had never won a national-level archery event until the Olympic Trials that year and she had to do most of her practicing for that in the family driveway.

At first, Williams was not bedazzled by his pupil. "Her arrows were almost turning somersaults," he recalled later. But his tips turned to bull's eyes.

Suddenly the 22-year-old small town girl found herself in tiny Joliette, Quebec, 40 miles outside Montreal in a field of 28 female archers including the heavily-favored Russian pair of Valencian Kovpan and Zebiniso Rustamova with Olympic medals at stake.

The four-day competition called for two international rounds of 36 arrows each at 70, 60, 50 and 30 meters for each round.

"For four days before the first day of shooting, I was really a basket case," Luann said afterward. "I was all nerves—I didn't eat, I didn't sleep. I wandered around and was miserable, although I managed to shoot well."

At the end of the first day Ryon was seventh. Williams' instructions: Calm down. Concentrate. Make quicker releases.

A disbelieving Luann wound up 33 points ahead of Kovpan, the silver medalist, with a world record aggregate point total of 2,499. So exhilarated was Ryon that within days she won the U.S. nationals and the Championship of The Americas.

Later in her career Luann said that some day she wanted to be "remembered as a happy archer who brought a smile to tournament archery."

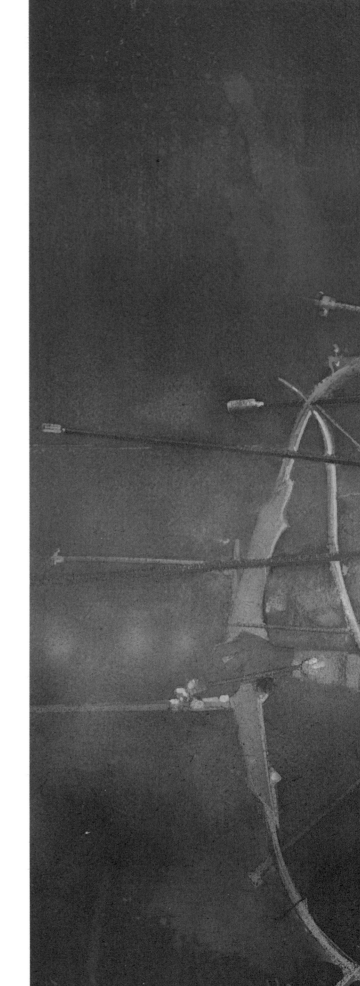

Archer Luann Ryon displayed all-important concentration during the 1976 Olympics.

When Al Oerter stepped to the top of the victory platform at the rain-soaked Estadio Olympico in 1968, claps of thunder and bolts of lightning pierced the Mexico City evening air. It was as if the Greek gods were applauding.

At 32, the computer analyst from Long Island had just won a gold medal in the same event in his fourth consecutive Olympic Games appearance. No athlete from any nation in any sport has matched that.

What's more, Oerter did it in the discus throw— the mostly highly-prized and honored of all the ancient Greek Olympic events.

In 1956 at Melbourne, 1960 at Rome, 1964 at Tokyo and again at Mexico City, he was the under-dog. Each time he had not won the U.S. Olympic Trials, he did not hold the world record going into the Olympics and he was not the favorite because he faced bigger rivals with more impressive creden-tials.

Yet this most durable, indomitable athlete didn't just win. He shattered the Olympic record each time in accomplishing his self-imposed mission.

In a sense, every contest was a golden moment to Alfred Oerter. He had four of them in the Olympics yet none said more about the iron will of the man than his pain-wracked performance in Japan.

For months in 1964 Oerter had worn a specially made neck harness because of a chronic cervical disc problem. Yet his carefully-programmed prepara-tions were on target with his own estimate that it would take a 200-foot throw to win the Olympics.

Al Oerter, the first athlete ever to win gold medals in the same event at four successive Olympic Games, captured the discus throw title in 1956, 1960, 1964 and 1968.

The favorite was Czechoslovakia's Ludvik Danek whose world record throw of 211 feet, 9 inches was more than 5½ feet further than Oerter's best. And American Jay Silvester had won the U.S. Trials.

Just six days before the discus competition during a muddy practice session, Oerter fell heavily, tearing cartileges off his rib cage. U.S. team physicians shook their heads at Oerter's chances of competing.

Oerter's response?: "These are the Olympics. You die before you quit."

On the Day of Decision, Al showed up for the morning qualifying round with his ribs heavily taped, encased in an ice pack and armed with vials of ammonia to fight off nausea.

On his first practice throw Oerter doubled up in pain. "I was thinking of dropping out," he admitted later. "Then the competition came, the adrenalin started flowing and everything worked."

He made it to the final on one good qualifying toss of 198-7½.

Facing his fifth try in the afternoon showdown, Oerter was seven feet behind Danek, the leader. Al's first four efforts had been hampered by the tight wrapping around his ribs.

"I told myself this was the Olympic Games and to forget everything else and get one really good throw," Oerter recalled. "I just tried to hop into some kind of position so I could take an arm rip at it. I couldn't use a body throw at all. I hopped around and hammered it."

That fifth throw traveled 200-1½—compared to Danek's best of 198-6½.

"Don't play this up like I'm a hero," Al told the press. "But I really gutted this one out."

Four years later, Danek was the world record holder, Silvester had authored a pending world mark of 224-5 and Lothar Milde of East Germany was consistently around 205 feet.

Oerter had worked to peak for Mexico City's high altitude. When the finals were delayed for an hour by rain, Oerter relaxed by playing catch with a discus while his competitors grew tense. His first throw was 202-8, then he scratched before unleashing a mighty toss of 212-6½.

Milde and Danek each surpassed 206 for a 2-3 finish while Silvester, fouling on three of six tries, could not top 202-8.

As a 6-foot-4, 230 pound University of Kansas undergraduate, Oerter first qualified for the Olympics when his best throw in the U.S. Trials, which appeared to be headed out of bounds, just did curve back in bounds before landing.

The favorite at Melbourne in 1956 was Fortune Gordien, the huge, smooth-throwing cattleman from Oregon attending the University of Minnesota. But on his very first throw Oerter registered an Olympic record 184-10½ and no one else came close.

At Rome in 1960 Oerter got a little help from a friend. Fellow American Rink Babka and Polish world record holder Edmund Piatowski headed the field along with Al. Bothered by the heat, Oerter was having trouble in practice. Babka told him to carry the discus higher in his throws and, after making the adjustment, the latter tossed for the distance of 194-2 and the gold medal.

When he temporarily retired from competition after his 1968 triumph, Oerter reflected on his remarkable Olympic career:

"I competed because I loved competition. It was easy because I won the big ones, but I like to think I would have wanted to continue just for the joy of competition even without winning.

"There is nothing comparable to the Olympics. You work and sacrifice for years trying to bring out the best in yourself and have to come up to the test of the best in one day, when you're so scared you're sick and shaking.

"It doesn't matter that my event is not a popular one . . . that gold medal is sufficient recognition of all the pain you've put up with.

"Of course, I am proud of my four straight Olympic victories. After all, no one else ever did that.

"But I think I'll remember best the Olympic experience itself, all those athletes from all over the world, coming together not only to compete but to make friends, meet one another, and learn to love."

By his own admission, Paul Elvström was 'word blind.' "I can't read and I can't write." For him, school was a throbbing headache.

But the doughty Dane more than compensated with an overpowering will to succeed. "In everything, I want to be the best," he said. In Olympic yachting, Elvström won four gold medals to prove his point. He stubbornly, though barely, staved off a nervous breakdown to capture No. 4.

Raised in a house on the sea wall overlooking The Sound separating Denmark from Sweden, Elvström loved winning and the sea. When a neighbor bought a small sailboat and allowed Paul to use it, the son of a poor, widowed mother seized the opportunity to become a master sailor.

Many people consider boats objects of beauty. Not Elvström. The colorful, extroverted perfectionist saw boats as tools to be re-shaped and finely honed for racing.

Elvström was 20 when he won his first gold medal in England in the Firefly, a class of boat he had not seen much less sailed prior to the 1948 competition. What he showed the yacht racing world were the results of endless practice, meticulous mental and physical preparation, a conviction that a good start is essential and the ability to make quick adjustments to wind changes.

When he saw a photo of a Firefly, Elvström immediately improvised a cleat device to improve his sailing of the craft without knowing whether its use would be permitted. It was. Anything for an edge.

There are seven races for each type of boat in the Olympics, a combined point total determining the winner. Although he could not even finish the first race, Elvström mastered the Firefly, winning the final two tests and amassing 5,543 points.

Elvström explained that while others could sail faster, "I had much better tactics. I could also tack faster in windshifts."

The Finn Class, like the Firefly, is a single-handed craft meaning one person sails it. The Finn was the instrument Elvström so deftly maneuvered for his gold medals in 1952, '56 and '60. It is just under 15 feet in length with a beam of 4-10.

In fact, within a few days of his 1948 triumph, Elvström made himself a piece of deck or training bench as part of his 1952 Olympic preparations. He used sandbags on his chest and practiced hanging as much of his body as possible out over the side of the boat for the best possible balance.

Elvström started sailing a Finn in the spring of 1951. He was branded boastful when he told a pre-Olympic radio interviewer he was so well prepared he didn't see how he could lose. He was right. Relentless Paul had four firsts, a third, fourth and fifth for 8,209 points while runner up C. Gurry of Great Britain managed 5,449.

In Australia, Elvström had one bad race but won five of seven to easily out-distance Andre Nelis of Belgium.

Although he once confided to his brother he wanted to win six gold medals, Elvström just did make the fourth, not because of pressure from without but from within.

Knowing the winds would be light off Naples for the 1960 Olympics, Paul undertook a special training program to lose 10 pounds for improved speed.

After five races, Elvström had won two, finished second once and fifth twice. The night before his sixth race he became very ill due to nerves and unfamiliar food, fell unconscious and had to be dragged into bed. The next morning he felt "awful but I had to go out and then as the gun fired I felt better."

He won the race. "Afterward I knew I had won the gold medal but I was feeling so ill and my nerves were so bad that I could not start in the last race," he said.

Nevertheless Elvström had 8,171 points to 6,520 for Russia's Alexander Chuchelov.

Elvström did not race again for three and a half years with one exception.

But the man who built an international reputation making sails and building pleasure craft had left an imprint of unmatched skill, racing a wide range of boat classes throughout the world.

Denmark's Paul Elvström was one of the most versatile sailors ever in the beautiful sport of yacht racing.

Revenge can be a powerful motivator. Coupled with Daniel Morelon's athletic ability and talent as a master strategist, it helped the famed French sprint cyclist win two Olympic gold medals in 1968.

Morelon was born in the city of Bourg-en-Bresse, near the Swiss border, in 1944 during the German occupation of his country. A feeling of vengeance for the vanquished was in-bred.

Growing up in the post World War II years, Daniel embraced the French national sport of cycling as his own.

Morelon in the 1,000 meter sprints and Pierre Trentin in the 1,000 meter time trials were selected on the French team going to the 1964 Olympics.

As background, Olympic cycling is contested in two categories: track—raced on a banked, wooden surface—and road racing. Unlike the road bike, the track vehicle works in one fixed gear, which means the competitor must pedal at all times; has no brakes; utilizes very light, smooth tires for less friction and weighs from 16 to 19 pounds.

In Morelon's specialty, the match sprint races, two competitors spend most of the 1,000 meters matching technique and psychology to such an extent only the final 200 meters are timed. It is preferable to be behind, rather than in front, not only for drafting purposes but also because it is easier to "jump" or accelerate at a moment chosen to surprise the rival.

In Tokyo both Morelon and Trentin, each 20 years old, were outmaneuvered and brought home bronze medals. Italians G. Pettenella and S. Bianchetto finished ahead of Morelon although he defeated the same adversaries two months later in the world championships.

Four years later the French pair made their Olympic return.

"Mexico City was our chance for revenge," Morelon said. "We were 24, more mature, more assured, more skilled."

In a disputed semifinal match with a Russian, Morelon had to wait for an hour before his victory was upheld. Then in the first heat of the finals Italy's G. Turrini also lodged a complaint and, again, Morelon was judged blameless.

"In the second heat I was charged up and mad that the Italian had complained because he didn't have what it takes," Morelon recalled later. "I absolutely had to win the second heat to bring back the gold medal. I decided to lead the sprint in front. . . . The Italian tried to put me on the spot, but I passed cleanly and led the sprint. As the finish line approached, I said to myself, 'That's it. You have it.'"

Morelon and Trentin had each won individual gold medals, then combined to capture the 2,000 meter tandem event.

Four years later Morelon, by now 28-year old coach of the Paris Fire Department, won as he pleased in the 1972 Munich Olympics. Denmark's Niels Fredborg and Holland's Peter van Doorn and Klass Balk could not win a single race against the Frenchman.

Morelon finally had to settle for the silver medal at Montreal's Games in 1976, upset by Czech A. Tkak.

During his racing career, Morelon was six times world sprint champion.

French sprint cyclist Daniel Morelon (foreground) had the ability to win by close margins consistently.

Her nickname was Csibi or "Little Hen." Her style was left-handed and aggressive. Her chief athletic asset was that the tougher the opposition and the greater the pressure the better she performed.

Meet Ilona Elek Hepp of Hungary, the most heralded female fencer in history.

Only World War II, which forced cancellation of two Olympiads, and rules restrictions prevented her from collecting more Olympic honors. As it was, she triumphed in a hairline decision in Berlin in 1936—then came back 12 years later in London to demonstrate her competitive excellence and win a second gold medal.

A tactical error in Helsinki caused her to settle for a silver medal at age 45.

There are three weapons in fencing: foil, epee and saber. Women compete only in the foil, a thrusting device with a flexible blade and circular guard for the hand. Although individual matches began in 1924, it was Elek's misfortune that women's team foil—at which she also excelled— was not added to the Olympic program until 1960.

Four touches in the target area—the body trunk excluding arms, legs and head—wins a women's match.

An accomplished composer of music, Ilona arrived in Berlin fired by incredible determination. Movements which she executed poorly at times in practice she performed flawlessly in the heat of battle.

At the time, eight women made the fencing final in a round robin type of play meaning each contestant fought seven bouts. Elek was courageous,

Ilona Elek was so skilled she won her first world fencing title in 1933 and helped Hungary to the world team championship in 1955.

strong to the point of overpowering some rivals and smart enough to anticipate the moves of others.

In the showdown she met Helene Mayer, 1928 gold medalist and then-resident of Oakland, California, who returned to compete for her native Germany. A classical fencer and superb technician, Mayer lost to the 29-year-old who fought harder.

Elek, whose married names were Schacherer and later Hepp, in the final count had scored 6-1 in matches. Mayer won the silver medal because she had received fewer hits than Austria's Helen Preis, though both were 5-2.

Despite the major time lapse, Ilona returned in 1948 to best Karen Lachmann of Denmark.

At Helsinki in '52, she was 5-0 in matches before losing to eventual gold medalist Irene Camber of Italy.

From 1933 in Budapest to 1955 in Rome, she won 11 gold medals, five silver and one bronze in individual and team world championships. In 1982, she was elected an honorary member of the International Fencing Foundation, the only woman ever selected.

The most gold medals won by a woman fencer are four by Russia's Elena Novikova-Belova, 1968-76, three of them in the team competition unavailable to Elek.

Among men fencers, Italy's Nedo Nadi won five gold medals in foil, saber and epee in 1920—a record for gold in a single Olympics until American swimmer Mark Spitz captured seven in 1972. Another Italian, Edoardo Mangiarotti, won 13 Olympic medals, six of them gold, in foil and epee, 1936-60.

Bettering a world record is one thing, winning an Olympic event is another. The difference is pressure. Wladyslaw Kozakiewicz, a space-age Polish pole vaulter, conquered tension, his past and a hostile crowd to accomplish both in Moscow.

The effects of intense nationalism were so brutal that July, 1980 day at Central Lenin Stadium that afterward the 26-year-old physical education teacher felt his gold medal had been tarnished.

"All of us wish to win, but not at any price," he said, indirectly voicing a plea to give the Games back to the athletes.

Kozakiewicz was a pleasing fellow with curly hair and blue eyes who began competing internationally in 1974. By the advent of the Montreal Games two years later he was one of the favorites in the pole vault.

But a leg injury hindered Wladyslaw so badly he wound up a disappointed 11th at about 17 feet, 2 inches. The second-ranked Pole, Tadeusz Slusarski, won on the basis of fewer misses at 18 feet, ½ inch.

One of his nation's most popular athletes, Kozakiewicz refused to remain depressed by his misfortune. By the end of 1979 the 6-foot-1, 185-pounder was a consistent 18-foot vaulter ranked No. 1 in the world. He had already cleared 18-feet, 4-inches or better a dozen times.

The world record stood at 18-8¾.

Then came the dramatic two-month buildup to the mayhem in Moscow.

In May, Kozakiewicz vaulted 18-9¼. The following month Thierry Vigneron of France did 18-10¼ and, just two days before the Games opened, another Frenchman, Phillippe Houvion, cleared 18-11¼.

Not to be forgotten, the Soviet's Konstantin Volkov turned in a world indoor mark of 18-8½ when heavy July Moscow rains forced the competition into the Znamensky Indoor Stadium.

The Games opened July 19 and the pole vault final was not until July 30. In between, the competition—made smaller by multi-national boycotts—was marred by accusations: too much Red tape, too much security, too much pro-Russian officiating.

On the pole vaulters' Day of Decision, six men had surpassed the 18-½ Olympic record before working up a sweat.

As the field dwindled to four, partisanship among the 90,000 spectators got unruly. A pole vault competitor is given two minutes to complete a vault. Such technical skill is required that crowd quiet is expected just as for the golf putt or tennis serve.

As he had done at 17-6½, 18-½ and 18-4½, Kozakiewicz sailed over 18-6½ on his first try, a height defending champion Slusarski also mastered. The Russian crowd roared when Volkov succeeded.

Then the spectators turned on Houvion with such loud jeering and whistling it caused him to abandon one run with his pole deliberately, then make good at 18-6½ on his final try with only four seconds left on the clock.

Several times the athletes lost their timing in the tumult. On three occasions the public address announcer intoned: "Ladies and gentlemen, silence please."

When the pole was raised to 18-8¼, Kozakiewicz cleared with ease. Amid the din, Houvion and Slusarski went out of the competition, the latter to Russian shouts of "Bravo!"

After failing twice at that height, Volkov elected to make his final try at 18-10¼—and missed. At last the crowd became subdued.

Kozakiewicz made 18-10¼ on his initial attempt for the gold medal. At this point he made a defiant arm-gesture toward a particularly vociferous Russian jeering section.

He still had a point to prove. He cleared 18-11½, marking the first time since 1920 a world record was set in Olympic pole vault competition. He also just missed three tries at 19-1.

"The public was very bad," he said later. "It was like boxing. I didn't like it. The whistles were hampering our performances."

From 1896 through 1968 Americans had won 16 straight Olympic pole vault titles by such notables as Bob Richards, Don Bragg, Bob Seagren and Fred Hansen. The Rev. Richards won two gold medals and was also three times national decathlon champion.

When pole vaulter Wladyslaw Kozakiewicz missed a second world record (19-1) at the Moscow Olympics he said: "I was close. It will come another day."

Coach Hirobumi Daimatsu could have jumped from the pages of a Charles Dickens novel. Captain Masae Kasai broke off her engagement because of national priorities.

Both were key figures in an almost fanatical crusade to make the Olympic debut of women's volleyball in the 1964 Tokyo Games a winning one for Japan.

No sooner had the '64 site been selected than the host nation applied pressure to get two favorite Japanese sports—volleyball and judo—to replace canoeing and the modern pentathlon on the Olympic program. The International Olympic Committee decided to make the additions without any deletions.

The Japanese then embarked on a multi-year Olympic gold medal winning plan to capitalize on the quickness, speed, small stature and acrobatic ability of their women to more than offset the size, strength and precision of the Eastern Bloc countries.

The results produced power volleyball—tough, physically demanding, sophisticated, intricate. It bore little resemblance to the game invented by William Morgan in Holyoke, Massachusetts, in 1895 for exercise-seeking businessmen not up to the rigors of basketball.

Ten of the 12 members of Japan's 1964 Olympic volleyball squad were from the fabled Nichibo Spinning Company team of office clerks who lived, worked and practiced at the factory near Osaka.

Taskmaster Daimatsu, who first organized the

team in 1953 and was the plant's procurement manager by day, was the architect of a sports revolution by night. He forced his pupils to dive head-long for shots just out of reach to learn to cover more ground with their short legs. He taught them to return the ball effectively while falling in a somersault motion which brought them back to their feet ready to run again.

The girls did clerical work from 8 to 4, then submitted to bruising, non-stop practice from 4:30 to midnight, 364 days a year, all for an average monthly salary of $50.

Above all, the Daimatsu dictum called for self-sacrifice for the good of total teamwork and national pride.

When the taller, heavier, precision-drilled Russians squared off against Japan in the '64 women's volleyball final they faced a fierce, emotional opponent with a gravity-defying, eye-opening dive and roll technique. The daughters of the Rising Sun had their breasts bound with elastic for greater mobility, had developed extra spring in their legs, steady chatter in the backcourt and a five-year unbeaten record in international competition.

The Soviets gave the Japanese a tougher battle than usual but Daimatsu's coaching paid off. Countless times the home team feinted Russian players out of position and placed the ball perfectly in a 15-11, 15-8, 15-13 triumph.

At the next two Summer Games in Mexico City and Munich, the Russians defeated Japan for the women's volleyball crown.

But at Montreal in 1976, Japanese quickness, agility, shot selection and enthusiasm again prevailed. Led by the precisely coordinated spiking of Takako Shirai and Echiko Maeda, Japan swept the Soviets 15-7, 15-8, 15-2.

The 1976 Japanese women's Olympic volleyball champions won all their matches, three games to none.

For Italy's Klaus Dibiasi, the 1976 Olympics in Montreal seemed like déjà vu.

The 28-year-old platform diver, nicknamed l'Angelo Biondo (the Blond Angel) by his adoring fans, was seeking his third consecutive gold medal. And despite the extraordinary skill he had exhibited for so long, Dibiasi was apprehensive in the face of rapidly mounting pressure.

Italians were outspoken in their demand that their favorite son prove once again he was Numero Uno.

Downplaying the injury in public, Dibiasi nevertheless had such a painful left Achilles tendon he considered withdrawing two days before the 10 meter diving finals. He decided to give it one last try.

And there was pressure from American Greg Louganis, a freewheeling 16-year-old bent on upsetting the master.

It was as if Klaus was looking at himself 12 years earlier at the Tokyo Olympics. Back in 1964, as an incredibly shy yet talented 17-year-old, he had faced defending champion Bob Webster, a U.S. Army private. Dibiasi had led after the preliminaries and even after performing one bad dive in his anxiety in the finals he still missed by a mere 1.04 points in winning a silver medal.

Looking down from the platform nearly 33 feet to the water at the start of the Montreal final, Dibiasi remembered. After the preliminaries the introverted Louganis was ahead by a narrow margin.

Dibiasi summoned his courage and know-how, edging slowly in front of the California youngster after five of his last eight dives. Dr. Sammy Lee,

Louganis' coach and two-time Olympic gold medalist in the same event, had his pupil primed to perform his most difficult dives down the stretch.

When Greg turned in a fine inward 2½ somersault he crept back to within 6.66 points. But while Dibiasi remained consistent, Louganis failed to be as impressive as he had in the preliminaries with his forward 3½ dive.

Under the revised point system it was Dibiasi 600.51, Louganis 576.99.

Klaus had become the first diver in history to win gold medals in three Olmpiads, then announced his retirement from competition.

Afterwards Louganis was satisfied he'd given his best effort and the sympathetic Dibiasi said he liked his rival very much, partly because he brought back memories of the young Klaus.

"Getting beat by Klaus is no disgrace," said U.S. women's springboard bronze medalist Cynthia Potter McIngvale. "He's a legend."

In between his Olympic beginning and end, Dibiasi went to the Mexico City Games in 1968 as a university student. He built up an early lead and then with two excellent dives decisively defeated Mexico's Alvano Gaxiola, a University of Michigan engineering graduate. Dibiasi also won a silver medal in the 3-meter springboard diving competition.

At Munich in 1972, Klaus took an insurmountable lead on the ninth of his 10 efforts, a 3½ somersault, to win the gold again, this time from American Dick Rydzke.

The gentle, charming Dibiasi came by his swimming skills naturally. His father, Carlo, had been four-time national springboard champion, 1933-36, and was on the Italian Olympic team in 1936 at Berlin.

Carlo coached his son well. And the city of Bolzano was so thrilled when the young Dibiasi won a silver medal in 1964 it built him an indoor pool.

At Montreal while Dibiasi was playing out his final symphony of motion from the high dive, U.S. Army Captain Phil Boggs, 26, stationed at the Air Force Academy, won the springboard.

Other noted Olympic divers include Dr. Lee, of Korean parents, who also won a bronze medal in the springboard in 1948; American Pete DesJardins, three medals, two of them gold, 1924-28; and Mexico's Joaquin Capilla Perez, four medals, one of them gold, 1948-56.

Standouts among the women were Patricia McCormick, only diver ever to sweep both the platform and springboard events at two Olympic Games, 1952 and '56, and East Germany's Ingrid Engel-Kramer, three gold medals and one silver, 1960-64. Mrs. McCormick achieved her second 'double' only five months after the birth of a son.

In 1968 Air Force Lt. Micki King suffered a broken arm on her next to last dive, losing the gold medal after leading throughout. Four years later in Munich Captain King captured the gold medal that had eluded her in the 3-meter dive.

To crown his achievements in his 1976 Olympic farewell, Italian diver Klaus Dibiasi received a perfect '10' from one judge on his last dive—a forward 3½ somersault.

Gert Fredriksson earned the title of "The Kayak King." The Swedish fireman was such a skilled paddler he became a national sports hero and an international legend.

How good was he?

Fredriksson won six gold medals, one silver and a bronze in Olympic competition at the 1948 through the 1960 Games. Because of World War II, he was unable to launch his Olympic campaign until he was 28, losing some of his most productive years.

He also captured seven gold medals in the World Cup, many Nordic titles and more than 70 Swedish championships in both singles and team categories.

Fredriksson was so good that in over 500 competitions he only lost five times! And in each case he subsequently met his conqueror in a rematch— and won.

The term canoeing covers both canoes and kayaks. The kayak paddler, unlike the canoeist, sits in an enclosed boat, equipped with a foot-operated rudder, using a perpetual motion stroke with a double-bladed paddle. Exceptional balance and conditioning are essential.

How did Gert the Great become so successful?

A Swedish magazine once referred to him as a "trainaholic."

Fredriksson had strength, endurance, an iron will and self-assurance. He never felt he had outstanding physical features, however. It was hard work.

"For sure, I take after my father who lived to be 90 and who had not been ill for more than one week in his life," Fredriksson said. "But most of all it's the training. All of my active career I trained very hard. I did not consider it worth getting the canoe wet for less than 10 kilometers (6.2 miles), but often I did 30 or 40 a day. In that respect I was ahead of my contemporaries. For a while, people would train for just short periods. But time taught us that I was right. So today everybody trains the way I did."

The demanding 10,000 meter Olympic course at Henley in England in 1948 had four legs, two upstream and two down. A heavy downpour ended just before racing began. Because there were so many entries and because rules at the time forbade heats for the long races, the kayaks were sent off at 30 second intervals.

This made it difficult because the contestants were competing against the clock rather than an opponent they could judge. Fredriksson displayed such superior technique he posted the winning clocking of four minutes, 33.2 seconds in the singles event.

Subsequently, in the 1000 meter kayak singles Fredriksson spurted from fourth to first in the last 50 meters of his heat, then captured the final by six seconds over Denmark's Andersen.

Twelve years later, at age 40 in Rome, Gert got his bronze medal in the 1,000 meter singles. After 15 minutes had elapsed, he and his friend Sven-Olov Sjodelius from the town of Nykoping teamed to win the gold medal in kayak pairs.

At the age of six, James Cleveland Owens picked cotton in Alabama to help support an impoverished family. Sixteen years later, "Jesse" exceeded a boyhood dream and quietly destroyed the Nazi myth of racial superiority with a four gold medal performance in the 1936 Berlin Olympic Games.

Obviously the swift, graceful grandson of a black American slave had many golden moments but the most dramatic came in his best event—the long jump.

All Owens had wanted was the chance to compete as an Olympic athlete as he went singing, smiling and making friends through the United States team quarters just prior to the Games.

Meanwhile, 100,000 Hitler Youths lined Unter den Linden for the extravaganza marking the arrival of the Olympic torch as Der Angriff, official Nazi newspaper, slurred the 10 Negro members of the U.S. team as America's "black auxiliaries."

On the second day of competition, as Owens answered the starter's gun in the 100-meter final with a catapult start, Adolph Hitler and Propaganda Minister Joseph Goebbels were among the 120,000 spectators. A world record-equalling 10.3 seconds later German citizens shook off their brainwashing to hail winner Owens with a thunderous ovation. A nation, if not its leaders, was entranced.

Day three, August 4, was Owens' supreme test with multiple 200 meter trials sandwiched between morning trials and afternoon finals in the long jump.

As the lone 26-foot performer in the field, Owens was to get his strongest long jump challenge from blue-eyed, blond Luz Long, such an unheralded Aryan he did not hold preferential German rank as either a soldier or policeman.

In the trials each competitor got three jumps. Owens customarily ran through the pits in pullovers as a warm-up gesture. Red flag. He had been charged with an attempt.

On his second try, Jesse took off cleanly but overstepped the line. Foul.

"I kicked disgustedly at the dirt," Owens recalled later. "Did I come 3,000 miles for this? To foul out of the trials and make a fool of myself?"

At that point rival Long introduced himself and made the friendly suggestion to Owens that since "you should be able to qualify with your eyes closed" Jesse should draw a line behind the takeoff board and jump from there to avoid elimination. Owens was delighted, drew a line a foot behind the board and still qualified by nearly a foot.

After breaking the 200 meter world record with identical 21.1 second clockings in the trials and quarter-finals, Jesse returned to the jumping pit. On his second jump he set an Olympic record of 25 feet, 9¾ inches. Long duplicated that distance on his fifth attempt as both leaped into a strong wind.

As usual Owens reacted positively to competitive pressure. His fifth and sixth jumps successively improved the Olympic record to 26⅔, then 26-5¼. Long rushed to extend his congratulations, then walked affectionately arm in arm with Owens along the track. Luz was keeping Hitler waiting to honor him under the stadium.

"He was a wonderful guy," Owens recalled. "It took a lot of courage for him to befriend me in front of Hitler."

The two remained good friends although they never met again. Long was killed in Sicily during World War II after which Owens met his widow and son on a visit to Germany.

Although shivering in the twilight chill rain and wind of August 5, Owens won the 200 meter final by four yards over Mack Robinson—older brother of Baseball Hall of Famer Jackie Robinson—in a world record clocking of :20.7.

By now Owens was almost a folk hero, admired by German athletes and hounded relentlessly by autograph and memento seekers at the stadium and the Olympic Village.

Nervous tension was building. Outwardly calm but inwardly boiling, Jesse said "it made me very, very nervous" when 64,000 showed up to watch some trials.

U.S. coach Lawson Robertson said Owens "has done enough" when asked if he would also run on the 4 x 100-meter relay team. His pleasant, saxophone-playing hero's weight had dropped from 163 to 139 pounds.

But when Robertson heard the Dutch and German teams were clocking :40.5 in relay practices, he substituted his best sprinters, Owens and Ralph Metcalf, for relay regulars Marty Glickman and Sam Stoller.

Owens, as leadoff, gave the Americans a four yard lead. Metcalf's pass to Foy Draper came very close to being beyond the legal zone but the U.S. won in world record :40.0 time. And Jesse had his fourth gold medal.

In 1976 Owens received the Medal of Freedom from President Gerald Ford.

And in 1984 the street leading to the Berlin Olympic Stadium was renamed Jesse Owens Avenue.

Owens shares the Olympic long jump golden moment with Bob Beamon who at the 1968 Mexico City Games turned in a monumental leap of 29-2½, nearly two feet farther than previously recorded.

Jesse Owens was named the Greatest Track Athlete of the first half of the 20th Century by The Associated Press.

When a 19-year-old Red Army recruit pinned his commanding officer the first time he attempted wrestling, his athletic future was assured. By the time Russia's Alexander Medved gave a farewell kiss to the mat in Munich, he had won three Olympic titles in three different weight classes.

Homer wrote an account of Ulysses versus Ajax in the *Iliad*, and the ancient Greeks ranked the wrestler second only to the discus thrower in importance.

If Medved was not so heroic, the blond son of a Ukrainian forester had the requisite instinct, skill, strength, and agility.

Yet Medved's wrestling career began almost by accident. As a Red Army rookie he stepped forward when a husky lieutenant asked if there were any wrestlers in the group. Even though it was a bluff he quickly overpowered the officer in a demonstration match.

Within a year Medved was entered in a national meet and by 1961 he was Soviet heavyweight champion. He won the Olympic gold medal in the light heavyweight class in 1964, heavyweight in '68 and super heavyweight in '72 although most opponents outweighed him.

From 1962 through 1972, Medved lost only one world or Olympic title and that was on points, not by losing a match.

An Olympic wrestler normally fights six or seven matches with medals decided on a point system. Competitors are charged a different number of points for losing by a pin, losing by decision, drawing or even winning by decision.

A trim 225 pounds, the electronics instructor from Minsk announced prior to the 1972 Games the competition would be his last, then won a controversial decision over Chris Taylor, 405 pounds, NCAA champion from Iowa. Alexander breezed past his other foes including Bulgaria's Osman Duralyev, who finished runnerup to Medved for the second straight Olympics.

"Medved was without equal in the upperweights," said Bill Farrell, 1972 U.S. Olympic wrestling coach. "He was not wildly exuberant or as aggressive as some but rarely made a mistake. He was an all-time great."

"Among the best if not the best American Olympic westler," is the way Farrell characterized Dan Gable who blitzed his way to a gold medal in the lightweight division in 1972. "Not even one point was scored against him in the Olympics," Farrell recalled. "He was so far ahead he could have lost his last match and still won the gold medal."

Perhaps no one ever worked harder than the introverted Gable who won 181 matches in a row in high school and at Iowa State University.

"He was into training so much nothing else counted," said Farrell. "In a match, he came at you every second—working, pushing, tugging, pulling. Many opponents could not cope with him."

Gable competed in only two world-class international events, winning the world title in '71 and the Olympics a year later.

"Gable could have won other world championships and one or more additional Olympics, he was that dominant," Farrell said. "He quit too soon."

Alexander Medved, the shrewd Soviet wrestler, was intelligent, pleasant and never lost his temper. What he did best was win.

Equestrian events—testing how well a horse and rider perform together—have been an Olympic fixture since 1912. They include dressage, a formal competition akin to compulsory figures in figure skating; jumping and the rugged three-day event, each contested at both individual and team levels.

Jumping consists of two rounds over an obstacle course with scoring based on penalty points assessed for consuming too much time and failing to clear a barrier cleanly.

The charming, dedicated master of the classic art of show jumping, in which his nation has excelled, was the Federal Republic of Germany's Hans Günter Winkler. From 1956 through 1976 he won the most gold medals—five—and the most medals overall—seven—in Olympic equestrian history.

The winning Winkler formula for jumping was simple. Take an obedient, thoroughly-trained horse with powerful hind quarters and blend with a self-disciplined, patient but firm rider to achieve a smooth, controlled effort in which man and beast perform as one.

Teaching a system well suited to German nature, Winkler led his nation to team gold medals in the 1956, 1960, 1964 and 1972 Games, a silver medal when he was 50 years old in 1976 and a bronze medal in 1968.

Ironically, it was Winkler's remarkable half-bred mare, Halla, that rescued his one individual gold medal at the 1956 equestrian Olympics, held in Stockholm because of Australia's quarantine laws. Sired by a trotter, Halla had not succeeded on the race track or in three-day equestrian competition before being loaned to realtor Winkler to give jumping a try.

The team began winning international events in 1954.

Two years later, with Winkler age 28 and Halla 12, they were renowned.

At the end of the first of two Olympic rounds the tandem was in good position with only four faults. But at the one gate they hit, next to the last in the series, Winkler suffered an excruciatingly painful groin injury.

Despite rumors he was being forced to withdraw, an agonized Winkler insisted he be carried to Halla to begin round two. With the courageous rider barely able to steer, his mount took command and majestically cleared all the obstacles for the first faultless tour of the course that day.

Four years later in Rome, Halla helped Winkler clinch another team gold medal.

At the other end of the scale, American Bill Steinkraus climaxed an illustrious riding career by capturing the individual gold medal in 1968 despite the fact Snowbound, his nine-year old gelding, had gimpy legs due to tendinitis.

Steinkraus captained the U.S. team to a bronze jumping medal in 1952 and silver medals in 1960 and 1972.

Other famed Olympic equestrians include Charles Ferdinand Pahud de Mortanges, the Netherlands, four gold and one silver medal in three-day events, 1924-32; Pierre Jonqueres d'Oriola, France, four medals including two gold for individual jumping, 1964-68 and Major Henri St. Cyr, Sweden, four gold medals in dressage, 1952-56.

Eugenio Monti—the brotherly if battered genius of the bobsled—lived the creed: "If at first you don't succeed, . . ."

A convert from alpine skiing, the native of the tiny northern Italian village of Dobbiaco went to the 1964 Winter Olympics obsessed with the desire for the gold medal that had eluded him. Yet at the critical moment in the two-man bobsled competition, Monti performed an act of sportsmanship that enabled England's Tony Nash and Robin Dixon to win the title.

Ten years earlier, despite major cartilage surgery on both knees, the versatile Monti won national ski races in slalom and Nordic combined events. But the daring redhead became fascinated with bobsledding and switched his allegiance.

Quickly adept at driving both two and four-man bobs thanks to thorough preparation, nerves of steel and great reflexes, Monti steered his way to two silver medals in the 1956 Winter Games. His quest for the best was frustrated in 1960 when Squaw Valley, California, could not provide a bobsled run.

Monti arrived at Innsbruck, Austria, in '64 as the most feared man in the field backed by eight world championships.

As the prosperous British tandem of Nash-Dixon prepared for their second of four runs, they discovered a rear axle bolt had broken on their blue sled and issued a hasty call for help. Just as quickly, Monti removed a bolt from his own sled and sent it to them.

As a result, the Englishmen led at the halfway mark and Monti, with brakeman Sergio Siepeas, was third, despite a record 1:04:90 second run.

"It was jolly decent of Monti, particularly when he was behind and not ahead of us," said Nash, a company director.

Despite what they considered a mediocre final run, Nash and his brakeman from the Grenadier Guards held on to win. Faced with a rapidly softening course and a later starting time, Monti refused to blame the conditions. He said his bronze medal was the result of his own poor driving and warmly congratulated the winners by kissing both on the cheeks.

The '64 Olympics provided Monti's career low point. He was primed for the competition. In the two-man bob, the winners were fun-lovers who had not expected to win, had never finished better than third in a major meet and had arrived in an antique Bentley automobile with a bar in the back. Monti also had to settle for third in the four-man event.

He thought about retirement—but not for long. In 1965 he was the recipient of the first annual Baron de Coubertin Fair Play Trophy.

The beloved 5-foot-9, 145 pound greying sled-master achieved Olympic success at Grenoble, France, in 1968 under unlikely circumstances. He was in his 41st year and disliked the Alpe d'Huez course. He had survived a race car crash and had undergone two facial operations due to bobsled crack-ups.

Behind by one-tenth of a second after three runs in the two-man bobs, Monti and brakeman Luciano De-Paolis authored a course record 1:10:05 only to find themselves tied with West Germany's Horst Floth and Pepi Bader. The judges originally announced both teams would be awarded gold medals, then found a rule that sole possession of first place belonged to the team with the fastest single heat time.

After 12 years Monti had his gold medal. He got a second in the four-man competition, limited to two runs due to the danger of a sudden thaw.

"I'm done now, I'm satisfied," Monti said. "I'll retire peacefully."

The Olympics never had a more popular champion than bobsledder Eugenio Monti.

With nearly one-third of the 10,000 meter Olympic race remaining, speedskater Eric Heiden was tiring, his left arm throbbing.

While the sports world was wondering if the powerful University of Wisconsin pre-medical student could complete an unprecedented sweep of all five gold medals, Eric had yelled himself hoarse the night before at the United States' 4-3 upset hockey victory over Russia at the 1980 Winter Games.

Amid steadily mounting tension and media hype, Heiden had overslept, missed breakfast and worried. He began the most taxing 10,000 meter test worrying that he hadn't had enough competition at that distance of 6.2 miles.

America's reluctant hero, who couldn't get the privacy so dear to him, was also worried when Norway's Tom Erik Oxholm turned in a strong 14-minute, 36.6 second clocking in the first pairing of the day. Heiden went off second with the Soviet Union's Viktor Leskin, current world record holder.

The crowd at the 400-meter oval in front of the Lake Placid High School—including Eric's private cheering section known as "Heiden's Hellions"—noticed during the race his left arm dropped. It normally was at his side in the glide position to provide the minimum wind resistance.

"I said to myself 'it's too early,'" the gracious 21-year old, 185-pounder said afterward of the growing exhaustion. "Painful? Yeah, it was."

At the critical moment, Eric put his mental preparation in command of his wearying if muscular body.

Diane Holum, Heiden's long-time coach and 1972 Olympic gold medal winner at 1500 meters, favored a steady pace as opposed to unusual early speed. She used hand signals to tell Heiden he was going too slow, too fast, just right.

As he flashed across the finish line stroking relentlessly on his huge, 29-inch thighs, Heiden had been clocked at about 35 seconds for each of 25 laps. He had just lowered the world record by 6.2 seconds at 14:28.13!

Meanwhile Leskin had burned himself out with Piet Kleine of the Netherlands finishing second and Oxholm third.

Many spectators stood shouting "U-S-A" and "Er-ic, Er-ic!" but Heiden was so drained he couldn't lift his head on his victory lap.

"What surprises me is his mental effort day after day," said Holum.

In a nine day span Heiden had accomplished an incredible feat, equivalent to a runner winning a sprint, two middle distance tests and two long distance road races.

Through it all, Heiden never quite understood what all the public fuss was about. He had simply come to the Winter Games to do his best. He left the athletic world reeling from how good that was.

In a sport in which a few hundredths of a second normally are critical, Eric had shattered the Olympic record for 500 meters by 1.14 seconds, 1000 meters by 4.14 seconds, 1500 meters by 3.94 seconds, 5000 meters by 22.19 seconds and 10,000 meters by 22.46 seconds.

Speedskaters race the clock, two at a time. It's rare when the draw pits a contestant against the opponent he most needs to beat.

Yet in head-to-head confrontation, Heiden whipped defending Olympic titlist Yevgeny Kulikov of the Soviet Union by .34 seconds in the 500, Canada's Gaetan Boucher by 1.5 seconds in the 1000 and Norway's Kai Arne Stenshjemmet by five yards in the 1500—all of whom wound up silver medalists.

Just before the Games began, teammate Nancy Swider had said, "I know Eric can handle the tension."

Nevertheless, he was concerned about his opening race at 500 meters because there was less distance to adjust to an error, he was better at long distances and he had come off the week-long world sprint championships in Wisconsin and a hasty trip to Lake Placid.

Fittingly dressed in a gold suit, Heiden was in a close race with Kulikov until the final turn when he switched to the inside lane and felt "I got a slingshot effect that helped me beat him in the last 100 meters."

In his third test, the 1500, he slipped when his inside skate hit a rut in the ice and had to put his arm out to "keep myself up." Holum said the incident would have cost most any skater to drop from first to fifth place. Heiden still won going away.

Eric had started skating at two and competing at the age of eight. The son of an orthopedic surgeon-skier-skater-cyclist-runner and former University of Wisconsin fencing champion had finished seventh in the 1500 meter race and 19th at 5000 meters in the 1976 Olympics at the age of 17.

By the time he reached college, Heiden was putting in a pair of two-hour skating practice sessions a day, attending crew and soccer workouts, lifting weights, doing sprint and cross-country running as well as jogging up stadium steps, not to mention bike racing.

Going to Lake Placid, Heiden had already been the subject of magazine cover stories and a Norwegian biography. But he had his life in perspective.

"I don't want people to put me on a pedestal," he said. "I'd be uptight if people were always praising me and stuff like that."

Terry McDermott, 1964 gold medalist at 500 meters, called speedskater Eric Heiden "the best who ever skated."

On Valentine's Day, 1984, the Seraphs of Nottingham—a 'perfect' English couple named Jayne Torvill and Christopher Dean—reshaped the sport of ice dancing with a glittering Olympic gold medal performance in Sarajevo, Yugoslavia.

The innovative twosome, who had worked like the devil and skated like angels, achieved the highest scores ever awarded in any international figure skating competition. They capped nine years of effort with an exquisite if tradition-breaking performance to the music of Ravel's "Bolero." It brought an overflow Zetra Arena crowd to its feet, captured the hearts of a world-wide television audience and convinced the judges their artistry was flawless.

Nine judges. Nine perfect scores of 6.0 for quality, unprecedented in Olympic history. Three judges also awarded 6.0s for technical merit, or difficulty, while the other six voted 5.9s for the British national idols' free skating, which accounts for half of the competitors' final score.

If it had been a game, it would have been a rout.

While the crowd shouted its appreciation at the lavender and purple-clad Britons, Dick Button, two-time men's Olympic champion, called their performance "a beautiful emotional experience."

"This is it, the pinnacle," Dean said afterward.

Dancing crisply and athletically to Russian folk music, Natalia Bestemianova and Andrei Bukin of the Soviet Union were good enough to win the gold under other conditions. But facing "T & D" they were like a runner being lapped by a rival.

Never before had 6.0 scores been awarded in the compulsory and original set pattern portions of Olympic ice dancing. Torvill and Dean collected three and four, respectively, in those categories.

Never before had T & D received a 6.0 for technical merit in free skating.

Never before had a couple received 19 perfect scores in a single competition, the highest previous being 11 awarded to Torvill and Dean in the 1984 European championships.

Yet the 26-year old once bored insurance clerk and 25-year old ex-rookie lawman from the land of lace, smog and Robin Hood gambled with creativity in their free skating.

Traditionally, judges look for three or four distinct changes in tempo in the free skating. T & D, pioneering a switch from what was once ballroom dancing on ice, stuck with a single selection—the "Bolero"—executing it with such finely-tuned precision and grace the judges were won over. America's Michael Siebert and Judy Blumberg tried a similar approach but were edged by two-tenths of a point for the bronze medal by Russia's Marina Klimova and Sergei Ponomarenko.

Subjects of a best-selling book, hounded incessantly by a nation full of fans and admittedly feeling the pressures of overwhelming public expectations and their personal goals, Torvill and Dean trained in the comparative obscurity of Oberstdorf, West Germany, high in the Bavarian Alps.

Success was not always theirs. Before teaming in 1975, the 5-foot ½ inch Torvill had been a failure as a pairs skater. And the dimpled, 5-foot 10 inch 155 pound Dean had broken a leg crashing into a skating rink barrier.

As an ice dancing team the chemistry worked. Dean is an artistic man of many moods, an innovative choreographer who is quick to anger. Torvill is steady, phlegmatic, fearless and adventuresome.

While Princess Anne of Great Britain watched at the Zetra, they wove magic on skates.

It was David versus Goliath played out on the ice at the 1980 Lake Placid Winter Games.

The underdog was a pick-up American hockey team of college kids and obscure amateurs, one of the youngest in Olympic history. It had been seeded seventh in a field of 12.

The overwhelming favorite from the Soviet Union—carefully culled from the finest talent of the Central Red Army, Dynamo and Moscow Wings clubs—was one of the best squads ever assembled. Led by proud, two-time gold medal winning goal tender Vladislav Tretyak, it had humiliated the professional National Hockey League All Stars a year earlier and whipped the same U.S. national team 10-3 just 72 hours before the Games began.

Set against a backdrop of American hostages being held in Iran and a Russian presence in Afghanistan, the confrontation became as inevitable as the Games unfolded as it had seemed improbable beforehand. The result was a most dramatic golden moment.

When coach Herb Brooks assembled the American team he warned: "You'd better report with a hard hat and a lunch pail." At Lake Placid he told the press: "My players are tired of hearing me say it but I have to keep telling them we don't have the talent to win games here. We have to do it on work, cohesion and rhythm."

A motivator and disciplinarian, Brooks emphasized speed, clever passing and puck control as opposed to the old American approach of dumping the puck into the rival's zone and chasing it. He hammered a group of good individual skaters into a solid unit. Even when the players became annoyed with him that, too, brought them closer together.

Before the final Olympic tune-up game at New York's Madison Square Garden against the Soviets, Brooks told the squad: "You should understand the lessons of history. The Russians are doing everything in their power to show that their way of life is a good way of life, and they are doing it through the vehicle of a sports team. We don't have to do that."

After the Russians breezed to victory Brooks was satisfied "we needed a good kicking to bring us down to earth." Soviet coach Viktor Tikhonov was suspicious: "We've got a feeling they have a lot in reserve."

If the Americans couldn't finish as one of the top two teams in their division they couldn't make the medal round in the Games. Trailing Sweden 2-1 with less than a minute left in the opener, the U.S. pulled goal tender Jim Craig in favor of a sixth skater. Twenty-seven seconds from the finish Bill Baker from the University of Minnesota blasted a 55-foot shot through a maze of bodies to salvage a 2-2 tie.

Midway through the 1980 Winter Games, a National Hockey League executive said: "The Americans skate as good as any team I've seen in a long time." After their stunning upset of the Russians, the Soviets had to agree.

Meanwhile Russia crushed Japan 16-0.

Brooks maintained U.S. gold medal chances were "slim and none," adding he'd be pleased with fifth or sixth place if the team played well.

Tickets for America's pivotal Game No. 2 against second-seeded Czechoslovakia, listed for $33.60, were going for as little as $4.00 on the streets of the storm-bound, traffic-snarled mountain village. Those who showed up marveled at the aggressive, swarming style of the upstarts who stunned the seasoned Czechs 7-3.

Down 1-0 early, the Americans shook off the jitters, gaining confidence as they worked the puck more patiently and carefully for better shots.

Goalie Craig from Boston University, nervous a few weeks before the Games, now provided the steady hand and psychological lift. He reminded teammates "if we can hold an opponent to three goals or less anything can happen."

The most accomplished U.S. skater was Mark Johnson from the University of Wisconsin who had played pee wee hockey with speedskater Eric Heiden.

In succeeding games, the "home" team battled its way into the medal round by defeating Norway 5-1, after trailing 1-0; Rumania 7-2 and West Germany 4-2, rallying from a 2-0 deficit.

Suddenly the unlikely showdown with the Russians was a reality.

Brooks had preached "we cannot stand in awe" of the Soviet juggernaut which had won four successive Olympic gold medals and five of the last six. He had encouraged a fearless, almost irreverent attitude, joking good-naturedly that Russian Captain Boris Mikhailov resembled oldtime American comic Stan Laurel.

Now $67.40 tickets were being scalped for as much as $340.

In the pre-game dressing room the coach read to his players from a yellow slip of paper: "You were born to be a player. You were meant to be here."

The atmosphere was electric in the Olympic Field House, jammed by 10,000 spectators including 1,500 standees. The emotion was volcanic.

As planned, the Americans kept up steady pressure on the Soviets with jarring body checks and intricate offensive patterns yet as time was running out in the first period they were in a familiar situation —behind, 2-1.

Dave Christian unleashed a 100-foot slap shot which Tretyak, unlike Craig's style of smothering the puck, let bounce off his protective pads. Johnson got past two defensemen, picked up the puck, faked a shot sending Tretyak to his knees, then poked a shot behind the goalie barely beating the buzzer.

Between periods a Russian assistant coach said Tretyak wasn't playing well and "my feeling is that he is nervous." In came alternate goalie Vladimir Myshkin.

For the Americans, the second period was a nightmare. Veteran Aleksandr Maltsev restored the Russian lead, 3-2, while his team had a player advantage; the Soviets outshot the U.S. 16-2 and Craig had to make repeated saves, some of them sensational.

"That's when we knew we had a chance to win," Johnson explained later. "Being behind by only one goal we knew we were younger, we knew we could outskate them and we knew we were going to break our butts to beat 'em."

In the final period the U.S. began skating better, controlling the puck, keeping the Russians off balance. Suddenly, while being pulled down from behind, Johnson tied the score on a Dave Silk rebound. The crowd went delirious, waving American flags and shouting "U-S-A, U-S-A!"

Ninety seconds later it happened.

There was a line charge. Buzz Schneider, the "old man" at 25, came off the ice early and Captain Mike Eruzione—the name means "explosion"—raced in to join linemates Mark Pavelich and John Harrington just as the latter fed him a pass. Eruzione raced to a point 30 feet from the goal and fired a shot, screened by Russian defensemen, that broke off Myshkin's pads into the net.

It was 4-3 and the crowd burst into a roaring tribute which lasted the remaining 10 minutes. Nothing else the Russians tried worked.

"They panicked at the end," said Craig. "I couldn't believe it. They were just throwing the puck in and hoping for a break." He also confessed to an ear ache resulting from the flu, adding: "I wouldn't let myself believe I could get sick. I'll get sick next week."

At the end, announcer Al Michaels shouted to a worldwide television audience "the Impossible Dream comes true!" U.S. players held their sticks aloft, wrestled and embraced in joy. The crowd shifted into prolonged pandemonium. Soviet skaters looked dazed by the outcome and spectacle.

Outside the arena chanting, singing, fireworks and searchlights marked the celebration. Across the nation, Americans reacted with elation.

However, the players kept the champagne corked. Like their championship predecessors of 1960 they had upset the Russians but not yet clinched a medal.

Trailing Finland 2-1 after two periods in the gold medal showdown, the U.S. pulled even 2-2 on an assist from Dave Christian whose father, Billy, had the winning goal against Russia and led the comeback against the Czechs in 1960. Johnson, son of the 1976 U.S. Olympic coach who Brooks said "makes our team go," assisted the go-ahead goal, then scored the clincher in a 4-2 triumph.

Later at a White House reception, President Jimmy Carter offered: "The U.S. hockey team! Their victory was one of the most breathtaking upsets, not only in Olympic history, but in the entire history of sports. You have thrilled the entire world."

One word described conditions on the downhill ski run that February day in 1956 at Cortina d'Ampezzo, Italy—treacherous. For the shy Austrian plumber there was more at stake than a record Olympic gold medal bid. So was Toni Sailer's safety.

Born in the village of Kitzbuhel, nestled in the Alps, Anton Sailer began skiing at the age of two. Through a combination of great natural ability and hard work, Toni had become a major international competitor by the time he reached 16.

When the '56 Winter Olympics arrived, Sailer, now a 20-year old, 6-foot, 174 pounder, was more than ready. He skied gracefully, flawlessly to gold medals in both the giant slalom and the two-run special slalom.

Toni faced the downhill test with the opportunity to become the first Olympian ever to sweep all three Alpine events. And the downhill was his forte.

"I like downhill racing best," he said. "In slalom, you have to brake all the time. I like to run free into the wind."

The bad news was that a storm followed by a thaw and then a freeze had left the downhill run—over two miles long with a 3,000-foot vertical drop—with a sheet of ice on the surface. In numerous spots, the ice had hardened into dangerous bumps.

These well-masked rough spots and mounds sent unsuspecting skiers hurtling into space. Before the day ended 58 of the 75 starters fell at least once—28 of them so violently they were forced to quit.

When Sailer's turn came to attack the "nightmare" run, he set out with determination. The first bump caused him to sail over 30 feet, his skis spread apart, on the verge of losing control. But Toni miraculously, masterfully recovered in air, landing upright and at full throttle.

For the remainder of the course the poised Austrian kept his skis firmly on the slippery surface, riding the bumps rather than being catapulted by them. His time of two minutes, 52.2 seconds was 3.5 seconds faster than the runnerup, Raymond Fellay of Switzerland.

"It was a murderous course," Sailer said. "I have never known such hazards. My third medal was the hardest to get."

Fred Rossner, Austrian coach, was not surprised at the outcome. "Toni Sailer is the most perfect skier I ever saw," he reflected. "He is the perfect athlete in perfect condition with perfect technique. He never makes a mistake."

An outsider—Zeno Colo of Italy, who preceded Toni as Olympic downhill champion—put Sailer's ability in this poetic perspective:

"He is gentle with the snow. He is never rough to his skis. His every movement is controlled, not by reason, but by lightning subconscious reflex. The language that the skis talk through the feet, to the legs and body, is a language unknown to most men and women. But it is the whisper Sailer understands best."

Sailer went on to win the downhill and giant slalom in the 1958 world championships but turned professional before the 1960 Winter Olympics.

Nevertheless, the rugged, handsome Austrian had been skiing's first true international celebrity, bringing glamor and recognition to the sport.

After trying his hand at acting, recording a song, managing a hotel and running a summer ski camp in Canada, Sailer strengthened Austria's national ski team as its head coach and manager starting in 1972.

His feat of winning three Alpine gold medals was duplicated only once, 12 years later, by Jean-Claude Killy on the familiar native slopes of Grenoble, France.

Sweden's superb Ingemar Stenmark captured both slalom gold medals in 1980 but was declared ineligible for the 1984 Games.

Andrea Mead Lawrence of Rutland, Vermont, became the first American skier and first woman skier to win two gold medals at the 1952 Winter Olympics. Marie Therese Nadig, Switzerland, 1972; Rosi Mittermaier, West Germany, 1976 and Hanni Wenzel, Liechtenstein, 1980 were able to match that achievement.

Toni Sailer tailored styles to fit different types of snow and slopes, carefully studied each race course and drank a concoction of milk, honey and sugar for energy.

Cross country ski racing is a gruelling test of an athlete's strength and endurance. Even his name spelled out Sixten Jernberg's qualifications.

Jernberg means "Iron Mountain." Sixten, the Swedish lumberjack-blacksmith from the Arctic Circle, forged courage, determination and stamina into four gold, three silver and two bronze Olympic medals in his specialty.

It was on the eve of his 35th birthday—February 5, 1964, at Innsbruck, Austria—when the slim, single-minded Swede with a soulful face enjoyed his finest moment in the Winter Games.

The "loner" from the village of Lima, about 300 miles north of Stockholm, learned skiing and self-reliance as necessities in the vast northland. Sixten began blacksmith training at age 14, lifting so much iron his muscular development was phenomenal.

But what the stubborn blond with the piston-like legs did best was work tirelessly to become a great skier. When he wasn't skiing cross country, he relaxed and conditioned himself by running or attacking downhill slopes at break-neck speed on the narrow, thin, light skis peculiar to cross country racing.

A perfectionist always working on some aspect of his athletic craftsmanship, Jernberg did so alone. He was outspoken about the folly of training camps which he considered too easy.

Jernberg won the 50-kilometer gold medal at Cortina, Italy, in 1956. He captured the 30-kilometer title at the 1960 Squaw Valley, California, Olympics but lost the 50-kilometer crown to Finland's Kalevi Haemaelaeinin by six minutes.

At Innsbruck it was to be a rematch in what Jernberg knew would be his final Olympic appearance.

Sweden's Prince Bertil was in the viewing stands at Seefeld when the national hero began his quest three minutes after Haemaelaeinin. The 42 competitors started at 30 second intervals in blustery, 23 degree weather to tackle the 31-mile, 120-yard course with its steady succession of hills. Although known in Europe as the "cross country king," Jernberg hadn't won a race that season.

But he had carefully planned his pace.

Sixten trailed Haemaelaeinin by 30 seconds at 10 kilometers, 55 seconds at the halfway point and 20 seconds at 35 kilometers. At 43 kilometers, where the course climbed from 3,871 feet above sea level to 4,438 feet—its highest point—the mechanical Jernberg passed the fading Finn. "I could see that he was breaking up," Sixten said later.

Jernberg swept across the finish line smiling, looking fitter than ever and with the comment: "Not bad for an old man."

He won in two hours, 43 minutes, 52.6 seconds—nearly seven minutes faster than his 1956 Olympic triumph and easily ahead of countryman Assar Roennlund, 18-year-old clerk and 1962 world champion at 15 kilometers. Haemaelaeinin wilted to 16th place, 8½ minutes further back.

Jernberg went on to win still another gold medal as a member of Sweden's champion 4 x 10 kilometer relay team in the same Games.

After Sixten won the Olympic 30-kilometer test in 1960, American team coach Sven Wiik commented: "Sixten's tempo is so fast that no one else can duplicate it. Where other skiers rest on the glide, he never does. He is already into his next stride. He always sets a faster, harder tempo. Notice that when he starts to use the ski pole, it bends like a bow. And he has the perfect temperament. He may look sad but he is not a pessimist."

When Sixten Jernberg beat Finland's Veikko Hakulinen in the 50 kilometer cross country ski race in the 1956 Olympics, his time was more than 43 minutes faster than the winning time at the '52 Winter Games.

Acknowledgments

Special acknowledgment is given the following contributors to this book:

Illustrations by Robert Peak of Scottsdale, Arizona, and New York City, who also designed the 1984 U.S. Olympic postage issues. Selected Artist of the Year by the Artists Guild of New York and elected to the Hall of Fame of the Society of Illustrators.

Foreword by James A. Michener of Austin, Texas. Pulitzer Prize winning American author, historian, editor and teacher. A holder of numerous honorary degrees, he is a member of the Citizens' Stamp Advisory Committee.

Sports narrative by Bob Hoobing, U.S. Postal Service, Philadelphia, formerly New England Sports Editor of The Associated Press and Sports Editor, The Boston Herald. He has also held an executive position in professional football.

Stamp design narrative by David Lewis Eynon, Philadelphia advertising executive, writer and former General Manager of the Philatelic Education Division, U.S. Postal Service.

Creative direction and design by David G. Foote, General Manager, Graphics and Design Division, U.S. Postal Service, Washington, D.C., who has designed or edited previous philatelic books, several of which won national recognition. He formerly was an art director for advertising agencies and corporations.

Art direction of the 1984 U.S. Olympic postage issues by Bradbury Thompson of Riverside, Connecticut, art coordinator for the Citizens' Stamp Advisory Committee, Yale University faculty member, book designer, typographer and graphic designer. Among his honors are: National Society of Art Directors' Art Director of the Year Award, the American Institute of Graphic Arts Gold Medal, the Art Directors Hall of Fame Award and the Frederick W. Goudy Typography Award.

Sports research by Joseph and Donna Turner and Marie Barry of Washington, DC. Stamp research by Edward B. Epstein, Paterson, New Jersey, Vice President, Sports Philatelists International.

Grateful acknowledgment is made to the following for permission to reprint from previously published material:

E. P. Dutton, Inc., for selection by Al Oerter from Bill Libby, *Stars of the Olympics,* © Bill Libby, 1975.

East/West Network Publisher for quotation by Al Oerter. Reprinted from an article by Ralph J. Fletcher, Jr., courtesy of *Express Magazine* carried aboard Amtrak. © 1983. East/West Network Publisher.

Farrar, Strauss & Giroux, Inc., for quotation by Bernard Malamud from *The Natural.* Copyright © 1952 by Bernard Malamud.

Gallant Publishing Co., Inc. for quotation by Luann Ryon from "Olympic Profile" by Jacqueline Farmer, February, 1977. Reprinted by permission of *Bow & Arrow* Magazine.

ICA-Kuriren Magazine, Vasteras, Sweden, for material on Gert Fredriksson.

Macmillan Publishing Ltd., London, for quotations by Paul Elvström from Paul Elvström and Richard Creagh-Osborne, *Elvström Speaks* . . . © Paul Elvström and Richard Creagh-Osborne 1969, Nautical Books.

The New York Times: For quotation from Harold Connolly in article by Steve Cady, October 27, 1968. For quotations about Nadia Comaneci in article by Dave Anderson, July 22, 1976. Copyright © 1968/1976 by The New York Times Company. Reprinted by permission.

The Putnam Publishing Group for quotation by Al Oerter from Dick O'Connor, *American Olympic Stars,* published by Putnam, N.Y., 1976. © 1976 by Dick O'Connor.

Random House, Inc. Alfred A. Knopf, Inc. for excerpts on Toni Sailer and Jesse Owens from Richard Schaap, *An Illustrated History of the Olympics,* © 1963 by Richard Schaap. Published by Alfred A. Knopf, Inc.

Sports Illustrated: For quotations by Edwin Moses from Rick Telender, "It's Been Step By Precise Step," *Sports Illustrated,* June 18, 1979. © 1979 Time Inc. For quotation about Luann Ryon from Herman Weiskopf, "Top Draws By Two Aces," and quotation about Klaus Dibiasi from Jerry Kirshenbaum, "Angel of the Tall Tower," *Sports Illustrated,* August 9, 1976. © 1976 Time Inc. For quotation about Sixten Jernberg from Roy Terrell, "The Heroes of Squaw Valley," *Sports Illustrated,* February 29, 1960. © 1960 Time Inc. Also for photograph by Heinz Kluetmeier as research for U.S. Ice Hockey victory celebration.

U.P.I. Photo Library for photographs used as research for Jesse Owens.

Wide World Photos for photographs used as research for Al Oerter and Klaus Dibiasi.

Additional sources of information:

BOOKS

The Olympic Games: 1980—Killanin & Redda; *History of the Olympic Games*—Killanin; *World Almanac & Book of Facts; The Encyclopedia of Sports*—Menke; *Encyclopedia of Sports*—Cavendish; *Purnell's Encyclopedia of Sports; Lincoln Library of Sports Champions; The Little Known Olympic Sports*—Jessup; *Highlights of the Olympics*—Durant; *Stars of The Olympics*—Libby; *American Olympic Stars*—O'Connor; *Olympic Greats*—Wright; *Show Jumping: The Great Ones*—Williams; *The Complete Book of Canoeing and Kayaking*—Richards; *The World of Archery*—Bear; *Archery*—McKinney; *The Story of the Olympic Games, 776 BC to 1968*—Kieran & Daley; *Olympic Diary, Tokyo*—Allen; *Track & Field: The Great Ones*—

Nelson; *Kyle Rote, Jr's Complete Book of Soccer; Soccer The World Game*—Soar; *The Encylopedia of World Soccer; Inside Volleyball for Women*—Peppler; *Olympic Track & Field (1896-1976)*—Track & Field News; *Contemporary Bicycle Racing*—Kingbay & Fichter; *Olympics, 1976*—Potter; *Olympics 1976*—Fulton-Smith, Graham; *Die Olympischen Sommerspiele 1972; Die Spiele der XVIII Olympiade Tokyo 1964; XIX Olympische Spiele Mexiko-Stadt 1968; Olympische Winterspiele Innsbruck '76; Olympia 1976: Montreal und Innsbruck; Olympiade Innsbruck '76; Spiele der XXI Olympiade Montreal 1976; Montreal '76; Nationales Olympisches Komitee; XI Olympiade Berlin 1936; An Approved History of the Olympic Games*—Henry; *Pursuit of Excellence: The Olympic Story 1980*—The Associated Press & Grolier; *An Illustrated History of The Olympics*—Schaap; *Guinness Book of Sports Records*—McWhirter & Cook; *Academic American Encyclopedia*—Princeton; *The 1980 Olympics Handbook*—Giller; *Lake Placid, the Olympic Years, 1932-80*—Ortloff; *The Official Report of the Organizing Committee for the XIV Olympiad; History of American Participation in the Olympics*—Louser; *Illustrated History of Basketball; Joies de la Bicyclette; The World of Gymnastics*—Tatlow (editor); *Olympic Games 1964: Innsbruck-Tokyo*—Lechenperg (editor).

MAGAZINES
Sports Illustrated, Time, Newsweek, Canoe Magazine, Volleyball Magazine, Yachting, The Runner Yearbook, The Runner, Gymnast, The Basketball Bulletin, Sport in the U.S.S.R.

NEWSPAPERS
New York Times, Washington Post, USA Today, Philadelphia Inquirer, Boston Globe, The Sporting News, Parker (Arizona) Pioneer.

Sincere appreciation is extended to: the staff of the Library of Congress; the staff of the U.S. Postal Service headquarters library; Maria Clement, Embassy of Finland, Washington, DC; Bill Farrell, former U.S. Wrestling Coach; Sam Foulds, soccer historian, Salem, New Hampshire; Britte-Marie Hagelbrant, Embassy of Sweden, Washington, DC; Sixten Jernberg, Swedish Olympian, Lima, Sweden; Stig Linner, Swedish Kayak Association, Farsta, Sweden; Kenneth Luostari, National Ski Hall of Fame; Eugenio Monti, Italian Olympian; Mrs. Toni Nett, West Germany; Ray Norby, Associate Curator, National Philatelic Collection, the Smithsonian Institution; Chaba Pallaghy, Chairman, National Division, U.S. Fencing Association; Bob Paul, Special Assistant to Executive Director, U.S. Olympic Committee, Colorado Springs, Colorado; Bernard Wagner, The Athletic Congress; Robert W. Wheeler and Dr. Florence Ridlen of the Jim Thorpe Foundation.

Two stock pages, with clear plastic strips for mounting the stamps and postal stationery, are included in this package. With the plastic strips open at the top, the stock page with the three plastic strips should be placed on the left end leaf. The stock page with the four overlapping plastic strips should be placed on the right end leaf. Each stock page has a pressure sensitive adhesive strip affixed to its reverse side. For the stock page to be properly aligned, this strip must be placed along to the interior edge of the end leaf.

Before removing the protective paper strip from the back of the left stock page, place it on the left end leaf so that there are equal margins on all sides. Once you are satisfied with the positioning of the stock page, remove the protective paper strip and press firmly in place. Repeat the same process, using the right stock page, on the right end leaf.

Using the diagram printed on the end leaves under the stock pages, place the stamps in the plastic strips as shown.

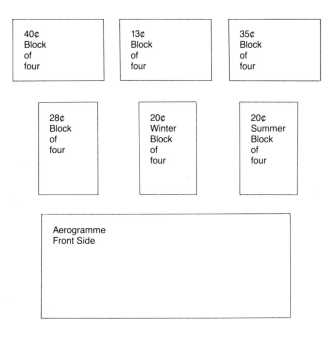

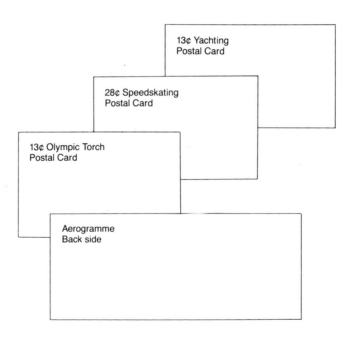

13¢ Yachting
Postal Card

28¢ Speedskating
Postal Card

13¢ Olympic Torch
Postal Card

Aerogramme
Back side